INSIDE

THE
COMBAT
ZONE

The Stripped Down Story of
**BOSTON'S MOST
NOTORIOUS NEIGHBORHOOD**

YOU
HAVE JUST
ENTERED THE
COMBAT
ZONE
YOU HAVE
NOTHING TO
FEAR
EXCEPT
FEAR ITSELF

INSIDE

THE COMBAT ZONE

The Stripped Down Story of
**BOSTON'S MOST
NOTORIOUS NEIGHBORHOOD**

stephanie schorow

BOSTON

UNION PARK
PRESS

Union Park Press
P.O. Box 81435
Wellesley, MA 02481

Printed in the U.S.A.
First Edition

Library of Congress Cataloging-in-Publication Data available upon request.

Book and cover design by Holly Gordon Perez
www.valehillcreative.com

Back cover photo © Spencer Grant.

UNION PARK
PRESS

unionparkpress.com
KEEPING BOOKS IN STYLE SINCE 2007

FOR MY FATHER.

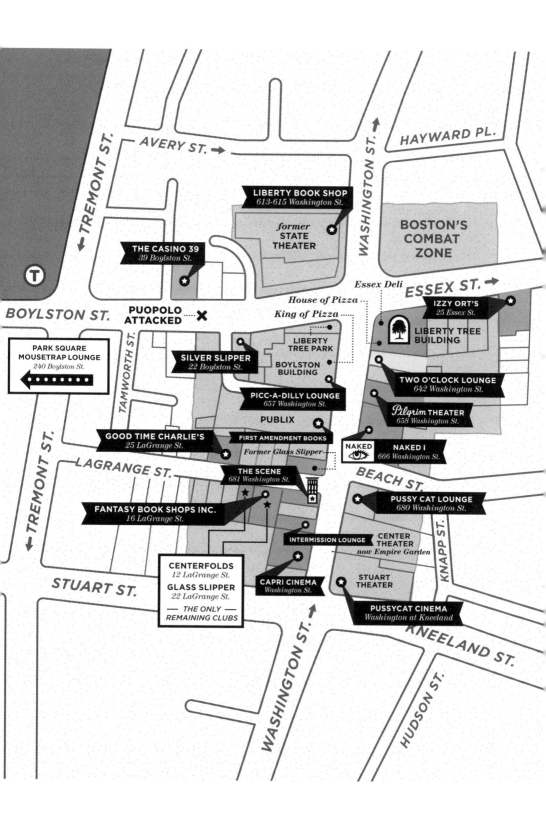

AVERY ST.

TREMONT ST.

HAYWARD PL.

WASHINGTON ST.

LIBERTY BOOK SHOP
613-615 Washington St.

former
STATE THEATER

BOSTON'S COMBAT ZONE

THE CASINO 39
39 Boylston St.

Ⓣ

Essex Deli

ESSEX ST.

BOYLSTON ST.

House of Pizza

King of Pizza

IZZY ORT'S
25 Essex St.

PUOPOLO ATTACKED ✕

LIBERTY TREE BUILDING

TAMWORTH ST.

SILVER SLIPPER
22 Boylston St.

LIBERTY TREE PARK

PARK SQUARE MOUSETRAP LOUNGE
240 Boylston St.
•••••••••

BOYLSTON BUILDING

TWO O'CLOCK LOUNGE
642 Washington St.

PICC-A-DILLY LOUNGE
657 Washington St.

Pilgrim THEATER
658 Washington St.

PUBLIX

GOOD TIME CHARLIE'S
25 LaGrange St.

FIRST AMENDMENT BOOKS

Former Glass Slipper

NAKED
👁

NAKED i
666 Washington St.

LAGRANGE ST.

THE SCENE
681 Washington St.

BEACH ST.

FANTASY BOOK SHOPS INC.
16 LaGrange St.

★

★

PUSSY CAT LOUNGE
680 Washington St.

KNAPP ST.

INTERMISSION LOUNGE

CENTER THEATER
now Empire Garden

TREMONT ST.

CENTERFOLDS
12 LaGrange St.

GLASS SLIPPER
22 LaGrange St.

— THE ONLY —
REMAINING CLUBS

CAPRI CINEMA
Washington St.

STUART THEATER

STUART ST.

PUSSYCAT CINEMA
Washington at Kneeland

WASHINGTON ST.

KNEELAND ST.

HUDSON ST.

CONTENTS

A 1774 anti-Patriot print depicting the customs commissioner under attack beneath the Liberty Tree. Courtesy *Library of Congress*.

INTRODUCTION

The Liberty Tree

. . . .

*Everybody who walked through the Combat Zone at one time
or another has left invisible footprints. Ghosts roam up and
down the street all the time.*

BOSTON POLICE DETECTIVE BILLY DWYER

A majestic elm tree once grew near the corner of what is today Washington and Essex Streets in downtown Boston. Its great height and wide-spreading branches made it a natural landmark for those dour but dogged Puritans establishing their city upon a hill. The tree was a century old when the Sons of Liberty, chafing at British rule of the American colonies, began meeting there to plan a rebellion. In 1765, they rallied under its branches to protest the Stamp Act, which imposed a tax on the colonies without their consent. From the elm's limbs, they hung an effigy of the despised British tax collector, jeering at the dangling figure. The Liberty Tree thus became the very embodiment of the American Revolution, a symbol of personal freedom and the right to defy authority. After the English Parliament repealed the Stamp Act, Bostonians flocked to the tree to celebrate.

So potent a symbol could not be tolerated. In 1775, the elm was chopped down on British orders.

For the next 240 years, the Liberty Tree lived on in Boston's collective memory, even as the neighborhood around its grave transformed. The open fields of the 1780s gave way to shops and commercial buildings, areas for business rather than fomenting revolt. In 1850, the Liberty Tree Building was erected on Washington Street near where the tree once grew. The building's imposing edifice, which combined

Greek Revival and Italianate architectural elements, was garnished with a bas-relief of the venerable elm. In 1887, a masonry and iron frame structure called the Boylston Building was erected on the corner of Boylston and Washington Streets. These landmarks—and the buildings springing up around them—were symbols of the city's progress in the nineteenth century.

As the next century dawned, majestic theaters opened up along Washington Street and the blocks came alive with entertainment: plays, vaudeville, burlesque, silent movies, and later, talkies. Department stores near the corner of Summer and Washington Streets attracted shoppers and bargain hunters. Near lower Washington Street, along Hudson, Harrison, Tyler, and Beach Streets, Chinese immigrants created what would become New England's oldest Chinatown. The branches of the Liberty Tree, were it still standing, would have sheltered a melting pot of Bostonians: Irish, Asian, Italian, and African-American.

Then came a post-World War II economic downturn, when investment ground to a standstill, Boston's population declined, and the city hit the skids. Downtown, bars still swelled with patrons, but the watering holes became dives, where soldiers and sailors gathered for booze and good cheer, which often turned to fisticuffs. Clubs that once hosted jazz and rock 'n' roll began to showcase a more lucrative draw: striptease. B-grade movies dominated the screens at once-grand theaters, and adult bookstores moved into vacant storefronts, including the (by now) dilapidated Boylston Building. The Liberty Tree Building housed a popular delicatessen and a pizza parlor and, following that, what was euphemistically called "adult entertainment."

By the early 1970s, the grave of the Liberty Tree was crossed by clubbers, men on the prowl, rowdy teenagers, pickpockets, tourists, hookers, and drifters. At night, Washington Street was ablaze with strip club marquees promoting girls, girls, girls. In the morning, secretaries, businesspeople, hospital workers, and shop clerks rushed past streetwalkers finishing up for the night and drunks sleeping off benders. Chinese residents moved quickly past the burgeoning pornography shops, seeking refuge in their nearby apartments.

City planners looked on in dismay. Something had to be done about the queasy oasis of sex shops and strip clubs in the very heart of

Washington Street, 1977. Courtesy *Boston Herald.*

the city. Boston's officials weren't the only ones wringing their hands over the X-rated sprawl; the entire nation was awash in what *Time* magazine dubbed the "Age of Porn." The spread of pornography into the mainstream was bolstered by a string of Supreme Court cases that barred cities on First Amendment grounds from simply shuttering anything deemed unsavory. Moreover, the lessons of urban renewal missteps were ever present: razing an X-rated area could potentially drive those businesses elsewhere.

With fervor both visionary and vainglorious, members of an unusual public-private partnership, the Boston Redevelopment

Authority (BRA), decided to confront the plague. They would halt the spread of the lurid, licentious, and vile with a social experiment as controversial as any conducted by Masters and Johnson. The city would zone the sleaze.

In 1974, the city's zoning board designated a five-and-a-half-acre adult entertainment district (AED) along lower Washington Street—a kind of neon cage for the bawdy enterprises already operating there. And for a few years, it appeared Boston would once again lead the nation on a radical new social path, one focused on a few grungy downtown blocks.

Today, pedestrians strolling by the gleaming office buildings, luxury condos, and trendy coffee shops that line Washington Street seem largely unaware that the area was once the site of the nation's most notorious adult entertainment district. The adult bookstores, peep shows, and strip joints are all gone—save for two LaGrange Street stalwarts, tucked away like cigarettes behind the counter. Students from Emerson College and Suffolk University rush to class from their nearby dormitories, commuters chug lattes, and playgoers flock to revitalized theaters on upper Washington Street, with blazing marquees that bathe pedestrians' faces in gold and red. They don't notice the ghosts of patriots and pushers, soldiers and strippers, mobsters and prostitutes, johns and drunks who once walked these streets. The shiny storefronts give no hint of the neighborhood's seedy past.

The emergence of the Combat Zone and the subsequent adult entertainment district represents a unique chapter in American urban history. When pornography was decried as public enemy number one, Boston attempted a solution that would have made the Puritans shudder. Across the country, communities convulsed with changing social norms—about civil rights, women's liberation, homosexuality, and open marriages. Boston leaders sought to navigate the waves of change, honoring the legacy of the Liberty Tree while clearly hoping that development would smack down the smut for them.

Today, many see the creation of an official adult entertainment district as a failure, leaving lives damaged or destroyed. Others point to the skyscrapers, the condos, and the Thai vegan bubble tea bistro and exult, "It worked out exactly as intended; it just took longer than anticipated." The establishment of such a district required vision and great political courage, says one city planner, adding emphatically, "It took balls."

The saga of the Combat Zone, however, is more than a tale of urban development; its history is rich with the stories of the people who worked in and visited the Zone. There was the exotic dancer known as "the thinking man's stripper," the former nun who became a lawyer representing pornographic bookstores, the tough but compassionate vice squad cop who knew every hooker on the street, and the stripper who put herself through graduate school. There were Chinese-American activists who fought to preserve their community in the face of pornographic creep and even development itself.

Writer Don Stradley calls the Combat Zone "a vortex," a place with the force of a black hole. This vortex drew conventioneers, curious couples, and young men—and some women—looking for a thrill because, he said, "If you went there, you would have a story for a lifetime." It was a place on the edge, sleazy and seductive, its neon aura and mesmerizing marquees casting a titillating spell. In true New England fashion, now that the Combat Zone is gone, many Bostonians look back with a kind of nostalgia, if not actual fondness, for a time and place that will never exist again.

TOTALLY NUDE

COLLEGE GIRL REVUE

UPSTAIRS
PEEK-A-BOO THEATRE
NUDE MODELS

Courtesy *Boston Herald.*

CHAPTER 1

IT REALLY IS A COMBAT ZONE

1950 to 1960

....

The barroom and bucket-of-blood days
have nothing on that street today.

MUNICIPAL COURT JUDGE GEORGE W. ROBERTS, 1951

On April 27, 1951, a short article in the *Boston Traveler* described how one Albert A. Silva, a former United States Navy sailor from East Dedham, was sentenced to a month in jail for assault and battery of a policeman. It was a modest punishment, and Silva got the worst of it; the assailed officer had shot him in the chest. Silva probably didn't feel a thing. By his own account, he had downed a dozen or so drinks at the Playland Café, a bar on Essex Street, just a couple of blocks from the site of the former Liberty Tree.

Judge George W. Roberts was not amused. "Much of the trouble is due to the licensees on this street who would continue selling liquor to a man as they did to this man," he declared. "It is a dangerous area and the services should put it out of bounds. This is not the first shooting down there. A sailor actually on duty there was killed. It is really a combat zone."

No one knows exactly how the area of downtown Boston near the intersection of lower Washington and Essex Streets—the place where the American Revolution began—came to be called the "Combat Zone." Likely the name was linked to the proliferation of military police, out to keep an eye on the sailors from the Charlestown Navy Yard or soldiers from the South Boston Army Base as they sought the pleasures of drinks and dames in the seedy bars. The nights often ended in barroom brawls. The drunk and disorderly were hauled off in wagons stationed in the area while the more sober were sent back to base.

Yet up until the 1950s, Washington Street—from the point where Kneeland became Stuart Street to the intersection of Winter and Summer Streets (the spot later dubbed Downtown Crossing)—was the city's main entertainment district, filled with theaters, shops, offices, and restaurants. By the 1920s, fifteen theaters in the area offered everything from serious drama to vaudeville to travelogues. If Bostonians weren't going to a show, they were shopping: the area became the city's retail hub, anchored by department stores like Jordan Marsh, Gilchrist's, Raymond's, and Filene's, with its vaunted discount basement.

A South Boston boy who would grow up to be the city's mayor loved walking down Washington Street with his cousin Charlie—a lead saxophone player for Louis Prima, Gene Krupa, and other popular big band leaders—to see a show in one of the theaters. The admission price included a movie screening and a live band performance. His cousin would take him backstage to meet the musicians, a treat for any star-struck kid. Some years later, he and his wife would dine at what he thought were the finest restaurants in Boston: Luigi's on Essex Street, the Prince Spaghetti House on Avery, or Jacob Wirth, the popular German pub on Stuart. Those memories were seared into the mind of Raymond Flynn, who served as Boston's mayor from 1984 to 1993, even after everything that followed.

Boston has been described as a city of neighborhoods. Beacon Hill, Back Bay, Dorchester, South Boston, the South End, and the North End each have their own character, quirks, and loyalties. But downtown Boston was not—until well into the 2010s—generally viewed as a neighborhood despite its thriving community of Chinese immigrants and Chinese Americans during the nineteenth century.

The Chinese community and other immigrant groups settled in the South Cove, an area created in the 1830s with landfill piled into Boston Harbor. It included both housing and a railroad terminal. Beginning in the 1870s, Chinese immigrants, many coming from the American West, moved into this housing. Some opened businesses, such as laundries and restaurants, while many Chinese women worked in the nearby garment factories. Fashionable town-houses dotted Harrison Avenue, but an elevated train track (which was used from 1900 to 1942) and an expanding number of garment factories made the area less desirable to well-heeled residents. From 1940 to 1950, the Chinatown population more than doubled from about 1,383 to roughly 2,900.

By the late 1950s, lower Washington Street, considered part of the South Cove, was a hot spot for popular music like big band, jump, jazz, and rock 'n' roll. Perhaps the most famous venue was Izzy Ort's Bar & Grille on Essex Street (later known as the Golden Nugget), which opened in 1935. Isadore "Izzy" Ort, a reformed bootlegger and legendary impresario, could have "stepped out of a Damon Runyon story," according to Boston jazz historian Richard Vacca. "He always wore a trench coat and fedora, smoked a cigar … and settled disputes at his club with a [large metal] flashlight." He was also known for his generosity to servicemen.

Over the years, the crowd at Ort's Golden Nugget grew rougher and tougher; in 1956, the *Harvard Crimson* helpfully advised patrons to "take a club." In September of 1964, evangelist Billy Graham, looking for souls to save, dropped by Ort's after preaching to a packed house at the Boston Garden. Graham had no luck. Yet Ort "loved Essex and Washington Streets. It was his whole life and the people who went there were his people," writes veteran reporter Bill Buchanan of the *Boston Globe*. Ort sold the club in 1969; by that time, his former neighborhood had transformed from a rough-edged stomping ground to something seamier.

The transformation had begun with the post-war slump. After World War II, Boston was enveloped by an economic malaise; investment in the city slowed to a trickle. The Charlestown Navy Yard and the South Boston Army Base closed, further undercutting the economy. Boston's population shrank from eight hundred thousand in 1950 to a low point of six hundred thousand in 1970. Helped by the creation of an interstate highway network, people were moving to the suburbs. In 1900, the city was fourth in the nation for banking; by 1964, it was tenth. Over a twenty-year period, virtually nothing was built downtown; you couldn't give away property there. The downturn extended throughout the region: In 1947, two hundred and eighty thousand

The Golden Nugget and the Playland Café on
Essex Street in the 1960s. Courtesy City of Boston.

people worked in New England's textile mills. By 1964, that number
had fallen below one hundred thousand.

To observers, Boston had entered a state of permanent economic
decay. Downtown Boston had turned into "a dreary jungle of honky-
tonks for sailors, dreary department store windows, Loew's movie
houses, hillbilly bands, strippers, parking lots, [and] undistinguished
new buildings," reported Elizabeth Hardwick in *Harper's Magazine* in
1959. Park Square, a block away from Boston's Public Garden, had shifted from an upscale neighborhood into a shabby collection of parking

garages and bars. The downtown was still a place for entertainment —that is, if you could handle the fights. However, theater lights were dimming up and down Washington. Television had changed people's entertainment habits; families were staying home instead of heading to the theater. In the early part of the twentieth century, Boston had fifty legitimate theaters throughout the city; by 1979, only four remained open.

The *Record American*, one of the city's several newspapers, took aim in a massive investigative series at the nefarious activities that were springing up on lower Washington Street. Beginning on July 1, 1964, three *Record American* reporters wrote story after story laced with the purplest of prose decrying the "so-called combat zone," where drinks were sold openly to minors on streets rife with prostitutes and where "homosexuals in some cafes and lounges" could be found. The series of articles charged Boston's licensing board with choosing to ignore the problems. On July 7, the paper printed a letter from an anguished mother to series author Jean Cole, praising the *Record American* for "exposing the filth and corruption in these so-called places of entertainment in our city." By August, the *Record American* was still reveling in revelations, hammering away at the notion of a modest Boston. "Despite protestations to the contrary, there is a 'red light district' in Boston," the paper reported, citing seventy-one prostitution arrests in the South End and the Combat Zone. Thanks in part to Jean Cole and the *Record American*, the label "Combat Zone" entered Boston's lexicon.

What converted the Combat Zone from a rowdy, rough neighborhood into an adult playground was an act of urban renewal, one of many that would reshape Boston through the 1970s. The transformation was an offshoot of a grandiose plan to launch a "New Boston." Like every road to hell, it began with good intentions.

CHAPTER 2

FROM SCOLLAY SQUARE TO THE COMBAT ZONE

1960 to 1971

....

The people who made Scollay Square what it was have not gone. They have simply moved.

"THE COMBAT ZONE: AN IN-DEPTH REPORT"
BOSTON GLOBE, **JULY 31, 1966**

Conceptually, "New Boston" was not unlike what John Winthrop described in his 1630 speech to fellow Massachusetts Bay colonists when he declared their new community "shall be as a City upon a Hill, the eyes of all people are upon us." New Boston would be "dramatically different from the shabby, stolid, and tired old city of the first half of the century," wrote historian Lawrence W. Kennedy. In 1949, John Hynes used the slogan "New Boston" to oust the primary representative of "old" Boston: Mayor James Michael Curley, the master of the wink-and-nod style of local politics. In 1950, the city's planning board issued its influential "General Plan for Boston," which proposed redeveloping 20 percent of the city's land area over the next twenty-five years. Thanks to the Housing Act of 1949, the federal government was ready to funnel millions of dollars into cities like Boston to counter urban blight and poverty.

First called "urban development" and then "urban renewal," the process was meant to retire dirty, old Boston for good—but sometimes at the expense of its inhabitants. The city cheered Mayor Hynes for luring the Prudential Insurance Company to Boston's Back Bay where the company built a towering skyscraper, which remains a landmark today. From 1955 to 1957, planners transformed the New York Streets, a section between the South End and South Boston, changing it from a neighborhood of crowded tenement buildings into an industrial zone. This "renewal" displaced immigrants and long-time residents, and the cheering was far fainter. In 1958, the Boston Housing Authority (BHA) began to raze the West End, one of the city's most crowded neighborhoods that housed a poor, multi-ethnic community. In its place rose an upscale housing development that was unaffordable to most former residents. The elimination of the West End would become one of Boston's most reviled acts of urban renewal with repercussions that have echoed through the decades and across the nation.

Chinatown, meanwhile, continued to expand. The Chinese Merchants Association of Massachusetts, founded in 1903, sought to enhance the community by building its new headquarters at 20 Hudson Street. The grand, stylish design, which incorporated Chinese features, was meant to symbolize the growing status of Chinatown. The four-story building took up an entire city block and was completed in 1951 amid much praise. That delight would prove short lived.

Spurred by available federal transportation funds, Boston city planners hoped to provide access to businesses and relieve traffic congestion with a new elevated highway that would run right through the city's business district. The intended path of this "Central Artery" cut off the North End from the rest of the city and sliced through Chinatown, demolishing everything between Tyler and Hudson Streets from Essex to Broadway. Construction began in 1951, even as Chinese residents, the Boston City Council, and others howled in protest. In May of 1954, the Chinese Merchants Association, fearing the worst, contacted state officials and offered to sacrifice its building to the Central Artery route to save more of Chinatown. So less than four years after its completion, half of the Merchants Association building was demolished to make way for the new expressway. That decision was seared into the minds of Chinatown residents for years to come.

Chinatown was again on the chopping block in the early 1960s when an extension of the Massachusetts Turnpike was built; sixty structures on Hudson Street were knocked down. Bostonians were slowly realizing that urban renewal was often callous to the very population it intended to help. Moreover, planning was chaotic and disorganized; there was tension between the city's planning board and the BHA, as well as between the suits of the business community and streetwise Irish politicians. A new entity was required.

With the support of Mayor Hynes, the Massachusetts legislature passed a bill stripping the BHA of its redevelopment power and created a new agency. On October 4, 1957, the Boston Redevelopment Authority (BRA) was formed, with Kane Simonian as its head.

From its inception, the BRA was an unusual institution, with a semi-autonomous, five-member board. Four members were appointed by the mayor and one by the state. Among the members was Monsignor Francis J. Lally, a Catholic priest and editor of Boston's Catholic newspaper, *The Pilot*. (The thought was that a priest could add a more human approach to development.) The BRA began to remake Boston, aided in large part by its unique mandate, which included both planning and development. The new agency had the authority to plan urban renewal projects and the power to buy and sell property, acquire land through eminent domain, and grant tax concessions to encourage specific development. This positioned it to become a more powerful and effective body, said Paul McCann, a BRA planner who spent more than fifty years with the agency and served as acting director on three occasions. With an entity like the BRA, Boston was the envy of every city in the country, he said.

With a pot of funds from the federal government, the BRA's cadre of expert planners intended to make Boston a prominent center of commerce and culture. Mayor John Collins, elected in 1959, was keen on the concept of urban planning. To accomplish this, the BRA "married academic planning with brass-knuckle politics," as *Life* magazine put it. The man who would lead the way was waiting in the wings. Edward Logue, the head of the New Haven, Connecticut, urban renewal program, was hired as BRA director in 1960 by Mayor Collins for a salary of thirty thousand dollars—ten thousand dollars higher than the mayor's. Both charming and manipulative, Logue cut a dashing figure and projected a tremendous aura of energy, power, and almost arrogant self-assurance, according to historians. *Life* magazine called Logue a "bold Boston Gladiator" and "the most successful redevelopment boss in the country and in almost all ways the most controversial."

The Boston Gladiator and the BRA moved on a project already in its preliminary stage: the transformation of what was then Boston's most notorious neighborhood. Scollay Square, just west of Faneuil Hall, was a warren of streets filled with bars, tattoo parlors, and burlesque houses, such as the Old Howard Theater and the Crawford House. Naysayers called it the "crossroads of hell," attracting "every sailor who could squeeze himself into a pair of bell-bottom trousers." It was also an entertainment hub, a place for both military men and their dates, men on "vacation" from wives, thrill-seeking debutantes, and teenagers sneaking out for a night on the town. Scollay Square "was an old and intimate part of downtown Boston where people went to forget their troubles, to get a luscious hot dog or cold glass of beer, to laugh at the stale jokes of slapstick comedians, and to enjoy the naughty spectacles of beautiful girls waving fluffy fans or swinging glittering tassels," David Kruh writes in his book on Scollay Square, *Always Something Doing.* Burlesque performer Ann Corio was a darling of the Old Howard among both rowdy sailors and adoring Harvard students. "The first row of the

theater, dubbed 'baldie's row,' would erupt in shouts of joy and pleadings of 'take it off!' but Miss Corio never did, at least in my presence or memory," said the man who would become Boston's unofficial city censor.

A rambunctious Scollay Square, however, did not fit the vision of a New Boston; rather, its decaying storefronts, sailor bars, and burlesque shows were a symbol of the city's decline. Plans were made to demolish its buildings and reconfigure its streets to create a sweeping plaza that would house offices for the city, state, and

The inimitable Ann Corio at the Old Howard. Courtesy of the Boston Public Library, Leslie Jones Collection.

federal government. Logue and Collins planned to relocate City Hall to the site and lobbied the federal government to change the location of its new federal building from Copley Square to the former Scollay Square. The belief was that this Government Center—to be designed by I.M. Pei and Associates—would attract private development to a rundown area. By 1961, the BRA had taken over all of Scollay Square by eminent domain and began demolition. In 1962, winners of a contest to design a new city hall were announced. Over the next five years, City Hall and the new federal JFK Building rose on the grave of Boston's battered but beloved entertainment district.

Scollay Square's demise was not widely mourned at the time. "Its death knell did not find us throbbing with nostalgia. Despite the yeasty vigor of its raffish throngs, the place was also mean-spirited, sour, brutish, and nasty," Robert Taylor wrote in a Boston newspaper in 1962. The Brutalist architecture of the new City Hall, however, drew mixed reactions. Some hailed the design as visionary, others saw a hodgepodge of concrete blocks. "It looks like the crate that Faneuil Hall came in," said one critic. Logue doesn't like Boston, another critic insisted. "He's pulling it apart." The ever-ambitious Logue was not deterred; he ran for mayor of Boston in 1967 but lost in the preliminary ballot.

The new City Hall was not completed until 1968, but Collins insisted on spending his last days as mayor in the new structure. Then the keys of the city were handed to the man who would occupy the mayor's office for the next sixteen years: Kevin H. White.

Intellectual, mercurial, and with a knack for hiring the best and the brightest, White led Boston out of its economic doldrums, but not without political and personal fallout. A son and grandson of Boston city councilmen, White grew up in Jamaica Plain and West Roxbury in a household permeated by politics. In 1960, he won his first election for Massachusetts Secretary of State, and in 1967, he ran for mayor, besting desegregation opponent Louise Day Hicks in a runoff. In the words of Boston College historian Thomas O'Connor, White "put Boston on the map," with new thinking and innovative development. Yet he was often seen as arrogant and a friend to businesses at the expense of neighborhoods. If Collins put the city on the road to "New Boston," White drove the last few miles.

The new Government Center succeeded in drawing investment to that section of Boston, but the wide, windy expanse of the plaza and the hulking City Hall are among the most disliked architectural elements in Boston today. Decades later, even Boston Mayor Tom Menino advocated selling the parcel and relocating City Hall. Scollay Square, by contrast, is regarded through a gauzy haze of nostalgia. But its destruction had another, unexpected outcome.

As Scollay Square was reduced to rubble, enterprises that catered to its crowd—sailors, soldiers, conventioneers, men on the prowl, and the like—proliferated on lower Washington and its side streets. Such businesses gravitated to the depressed, low-rent districts of Park Square and what was increasingly being called the Combat Zone. By September 1964, this area was packed with "the bawdiest, loudest gin mills in New Boston and they have been there since it was the Old Boston," according to the *Boston Globe*.

City planners had effectively cut the supply but they could not kill demand. A bartender would tell the *Boston Herald*: "When they tore down Scollay Square, everybody moved down here. The joints, the sailors, hustlers, everybody. It even smells the same." But it bears emphasizing that virtually none of the Scollay Square burlesque clubs and bars actually packed up and moved operations to the Combat Zone. Rather, the audience for such entertainment gravitated downtown; the sole exception was Jack's Joke Shop, which moved to the edge of the Zone. Scollay Square never had the nude dancing, peep shows, and X-rated movie theaters that eventually dominated Washington Street. A *Boston Globe* writer compared the process to squeezing a balloon at one end: the air just pushes out in a bulge at the other.

◆

In 1966, Italian immigrant Tony Pasquale bought the King of Pizza restaurant in the Boylston Building. For the next fifteen years, Tony—also known as "Tony King"—served cheese and pepperoni pizzas to office workers, commuters, moviegoers, cops, hookers, pimps, police officers, and late-night patrons emerging from the strip clubs. He chatted with Chesty Morgan when the top-heavy burlesque star wanted to get a bite after a show. He greeted the cops by name.

He often fed homeless people. He rose before dawn to make sure his restaurant was ready with hot pizza when it opened. Some nights he slept in the store after closing at three o'clock in the morning, when the last of the club patrons called it a night. His son, Mark, helped out during summers and after school.

Tony Pasquale was slightly built but tough. He once chased a would-be robber with a baseball bat even as the robber turned and shot at him. Mark was tough too; he never thought of the Combat Zone as a place to fear. Mark befriended and teased a cast of characters that regularly passed by. He harried hookers with questions about why they needed a pimp. He and friends hung out at China-town restaurants, dining while the rest of the city slept. He didn't frequent the strip clubs often, but he nearly broke his mother's heart when he announced he wanted to marry the stripper he'd been dating. The always-rocky relationship ended when Mark came to pick up his girlfriend at a club, chatted with another dancer while waiting for her, and got a beer poured on his head by his soon-to-be ex.

As Mark grew up, the Zone grew wilder. He watched it happen, not from a ringside seat, but from inside the show. Venues that were once part of a vivacious music scene turned to strippers in order to stay in business. Theaters that were gasping to stay alive did so by showing naughty films. Boston's economic woes hit downtown hard, and in porn, there was a sort of salvation.

The Silver Dollar, at 642 Washington Street, was one of the many businesses to shift its model to meet the increasing demand for risqué adult entertainment. A sailor's bar from the late 1930s to the 1950s, the Silver Dollar was known for its loud music and its even louder fights, as well as for nightclub acts. It once brought Evelyn Nesbitt to its stage, according to Richard Vacca. The bar later featured jazz performers like pianist George Wein and singer and guitarist Don Humbert, who wrote the song, "Meet Me at the Silver Dollar." Always a target for Boston's licensing board, the bar closed in 1954, only to reopen as the Palace and, later, the Downtown Lounge. Sometime in the 1960s, it became one of the Zone's most scandalous striptease clubs: the "world famous" Two O'Clock Lounge.

The Two O'Clock's shows became legendary in Boston, first attracting performers who refused to let the art of burlesque die. Headliner

Angel Walker, known as Satan's Angel, the Devil's Own Mistress, and Queen of the Fire Tassels, performed at the Two O'Clock beginning in the mid-1960s. She describes strutting down the bar, which seemed a mile long, in soon-to-be-shed sumptuous gowns trimmed in mink and ostrich feathers. "They hired all the biggest and the greatest [burlesque] features to work there: Alexandra The Great 48, Busty Russell, Chesty Morgan, and Gina Bon Bon," she recalled. A native of California, Walker started performing burlesque after winning an amateur strip contest at the age of seventeen. With her luxuriant brunette hair, green cat-like eyes, and a stunning 44-24-34 figure, she became a top act. "I worked the Combat Zone to death," she recalled. "I had a good time, but it was a hard place to work." The clubs also had private areas for more intimate shows where "you could show your hoo-hoo. I didn't want to show my hoo-hoo. They didn't have enough zeros at the end of my paycheck."

The Two O'Clock might have been "world famous," but it soon had competition. "Six years ago there was only one strip club in Boston," a Combat Zone bartender told photographer and writer Roswell Angier in 1974. "Now there are twelve."

Just down the street at 666 Washington Street was Jerome's Lounge, a rock 'n' roll bar that shifted from featuring music to baring skin. The place later became Jerome's Naked i and eventually just the Naked i Cabaret, perhaps the most infamous of all the Combat Zone's strip clubs (the Two O'Clock notwithstanding). The "i" was a play on the word "eye," and a large unblinking blue orb stared from the club's logo: a pair of upside-down female legs with that eye positioned at the crucial intersection. The club's particular enticement was a "Totally Nude College Girl Revue."

More and more bars began to ask performers to take it all off. Strippers became the featured ticket at the Caribe near the corner of Boylston and Tremont, the Living Room on Stuart Street, and the Intermission Lounge at 689 Washington. According to legend, the Normandy Lounge once featured a zaftig stripper called Sally the Shape who inspired calls of "Put it back on" by patrons. (Sandwiched into the 600 block of Washington was the Brewster Arms, a male boarding house that military men used as a quick-change spot to get in and out of uniforms.) In addition to Tony Pasquale's King of Pizza

Courtesy Angel Walker, pictured here. Also known as Satan's Angel, the Devil's Own Mistress, Queen of the Fire Tassels.

restaurant, the first floor of the historic Boylston Building housed the Picc-a-dilly (formerly the Tick-Tock, facing Washington) and the Silver Slipper (facing Boylston), as well as stores selling books, magazines, and other items that required brown paper wrappings.

The Naked i had a separate stage, called the Pussy Galore Stag Bar, which was used for more intimate performances. That was not to be confused with the Pussy Cat Lounge, which took over the former Novelty Bar at 680 Washington, or the Pussycat Cinema, a chain that moved into the former Stuart Theater space at the corner of Washington and Kneeland Streets. The marquee of the Pussycat Cinema, at the very edge of the Zone, was emblazoned with a black-masked, scantily clad woman with ears and a tail who threw out her hands as if to say, "Follow me, boys!"

Adjacent Park Square, with its bars and the nearby Trailways bus station, also attracted sexploitative businesses. For those who wanted sleaze with a side of Rat Pack relish, there was the Playboy Club, which opened in 1966. ("They had a great breakfast there," one Boston cop recalls.) Those who wanted steamier stuff could wander into the nearby Mousetrap Lounge and the Teddy Bear Lounge.

At first, music remained a core part of this burgeoning skin business. Until the early 1980s, many of the strip clubs featured three-piece live bands before ultimately switching to recorded music. Indeed, generations of young Boston musicians cut their teeth performing in the shadows of disrobing women and topless cocktail waitresses. A student at Boston's famed Berkeley School of Music recalled playing four-hour shifts of jazz, blues, and pop alongside other great musicians at the Living Room, all the while trying to ignore the strippers and sexual favors happening around him.

In the early days, the strip clubs also featured emcees like show business pro Bobby Burns and comics like Silky Silvers to entertain the crowds between dancers. Fledgling comic Jay Leno tested his shtick at the Teddy Bear and Two O'Clock. "When I played the Teddy Bear I was twenty-four and wore my hair long and we used to cater to soldiers and sailors and if I tried to do a bit about Watergate, someone would holler, 'Hey, shuddup about the president!'" he told the *Boston Globe* in 1983. Seediness begat sleaze. The magnificent movie theaters on Washington started to shift toward low-budget, grindhouse movies, then softcore and eventually hardcore porn. The Pilgrim Theater, at 658 Washington, once a thriving, legitimate stage and burlesque showcase, began to feature second-rate movies that gradually grew raunchier over the years. The 1903 Globe Theatre on Washington Street had a long history of presenting drama, musical comedy, vaudeville, burlesque, and films. Major stars who appeared there included James K. Hackett, Weber and Fields, Lillian Russell, Al Jolson, W.C. Fields, Abbott and Costello, and Gypsy Rose Lee. In 1947, the Globe became the E.M. Loews Center Theater, and by the 1960s, the Center was showing low-budget films like *Horror Castle* and *Incredibly Strange Creatures,* or skin flicks like Peitro Germi's *Seduced and Abandoned* and *To Bed or Not To Bed.* Not to be outdone, the State Theater, which was about two blocks away on the other side of Washington, got into the skin game with movies described as "Frank! Sizzling! And Torrid!" The Capri, next to the Intermission Lounge, also turned X-rated and, according to legend, achieved the dubious distinction as being the first theater in Boston to show the seminal hardcore flick, *The Devil in Miss Jones.*

Across the street from the Pilgrim was the Publix, another former burlesque theater fallen on hard times. Constructed in 1908, the thirteen-thousand-square-foot complex housed the Gaiety Theatre as well as stores and offices. The elegant Gaiety had been a popular vaudeville and traveling burlesque venue, and its proscenium arches featured oversized plaster heads of "Gaiety Girls" with ornate crowns. In the 1920s, the Gaiety featured black burlesque performances and comedians, one of the few places in Boston to do so. According to Friends of the Gaiety Theatre, a group formed to save the building from demolition, "The Gaiety brought the Harlem Renaissance to Boston. It was where Bostonians went to hear the new music called jazz." In 1926, Rarin' To Go boasted "the greatest array of white and colored artists ever assembled in one show." In the 1930s, the theater was taken over by E.M. Loews for movies and live entertainment. Eventually it became the Publix—and that "x" came in handy as the theater turned to striptease, second-run, and Chinese movies in the 1960s. A men's clothing store that had occupied a storefront in the building for decades was replaced by an adult bookstore.

That was another Combat Zone specialty: bookstores warning "No Admittance Under 21, Thank you." In 1961, Boston had only one

Courtesy *Boston Herald*.

bookstore that specialized in material that could be considered pornographic. By 1969, there were thirteen, all but three of which were in the area of lower Washington. This data was collected in a remarkable study conducted by M. Marvin Finkelstein of the Boston University School of Law, which was published in the landmark 1970 Commission on Obscenity and Pornography. Finkelstein and a group of obliging and daring graduate students carefully chronicled the proliferation of the archetypical "dirty bookstores" in Boston, trying to use academic rigor to figure out what spurred the demand for nude photos and seamy

prose. According to Boston University researchers, adult bookstores were uniformly drab and bleak, and window displays and store names gave little clue as to what was inside. "Material is simple, crude, and direct in its appeal." Researchers also observed the customers, recording estimated age, sex, race, and dress, whether casual, business, military, or "hippie" type garb. They interviewed clerks, one of whom said, "I'm not saying we're great social heroes but I do honestly feel that we're serving … a need … the sexual fulfillment of a lot of very frustrated people." Almost all the booksellers complained of police harassment.

Shoplifting also was a problem. When asked how this was handled, one clerk replied, "We break their hands."

The study also took note of a new phenomenon: in 1962, one of the bookstore owners installed a coin-operated machine that allowed patrons a two-minute view of a slice of 8-millimeter film for twenty-five cents. Such peep shows would proliferate: by 1983, there were 547 machines in sixteen bookstores and arcades.

None of this went unnoticed by the city's press. In 1966, the *Boston Globe* produced an in-depth report on the Combat Zone, declaring it to be a "Coney Island for the emotionally scarred ... The place for the emotionally and sexually deformed." With a tone both sneering and condescending, the *Globe* reported that lower Washington Street was now more crowded than any previous honky-tonk section of Boston—the streets narrower and darker, everything dirtier and more dangerous. The streets smelled of urine and vomit and "photographs of dancers on billboards outside the clubs are even less enticing in the sharp light of day, half-plucked fowls with thigh fat."

Even amid the bump and grind, people had to eat and shop. Throughout the Zone's heyday, luncheonettes, pizza parlors, liquor stores, clothing stores, and other businesses ran alongside the strip clubs and adult bookstores. Pedestrian traffic was heavy. During the day there was a steady stream of shoppers, office workers, well-dressed businessmen and professionals, as well as blue-collar service and construction workers.

Still, lower Washington long had an aura of danger. In November 1964, the body of a waitress was found beaten, stabbed, and stuffed into a sack in the loft of the once-popular Luigi's restaurant, owned by the Martorano family—a name that would become well known in Boston mob history. On January 26, 1966, eleven people were killed in a massive fire, caused by a gas explosion, in the Paramount Hotel at 15-19 Boylston Street, another indication of the area's decline. The once-respectable Avery Hotel began catering to guests who paid by the hour. The epicenter for prostitution became Good Time Charlie's at 25 LaGrange Street. There were strippers there, but no one noticed them. "Anyone going into Good Time Charlie's—it wasn't because the beer was good. That was a candy store and he was there to buy candy," said a police officer.

There was, at that point, no lack of law enforcement. "The place was loaded with cops," said Edward McNelley, a member of the Boston police force for thirty-three years and a former chief of homicide. The Boston Tactical Patrol Force patrolled the Zone, and that was a group of "big, big guys." Many bars hired off-duty police officers to keep order in the bars, even as hookers walked the streets outside.

By early 1970, there were about thirty-five sex-related businesses, including about twenty-six adult bookstores and nude dancing venues, all concentrated along lower Washington Street and in Park Square. The Combat Zone was becoming a world unto itself, at once sordid and tolerant, a community for those outside the mainstream.

City planners were increasingly alarmed. If Boston was to be a world-class city, how could it have an oozing sore of sexual depravity at its center? Morality aside, BRA officials knew the downtown desperately needed development. Planners were influenced by the "high spine" concept of Kevin Lynch, a pioneering urban planner and MIT scholar. In his seminal 1960 book, *The Image of the City,* he envisioned a corridor of tall office towers that would give a city a recognizable skyline. In 1960, the Boston Society of Architects issued its "Architect's Plan for Boston," which incorporated Lynch's concept.

As one planner of that era said, Boston's high spine would "kick off" at the Prudential Building and proceed through Back Bay and downtown, near its transportation lines, to the waterfront. The area of lower Washington was a barrier, "a black hole. Nothing was happening there," the planner said. This meant that private development had to be encouraged in the downtown area, which was as much of a challenge in the 1960s as it would be for the next three decades.

Something had to be done and it could not be with a wrecking ball. Knowing Scollay Square's elimination invigorated the Combat Zone, officials feared that the destruction of Washington Street's porn shops, strip clubs, and X-rated movie theaters would simply disperse them to other parts of Boston. That was intolerable. Already, "stuff was showing up around Route 1," a BRA official recalled. "Everyone was wringing their hands on how to control it."

Boston was not alone in the fight against sleaze. Pornography was storming the nation.

GERARD DAMIANO'S

DEEP THROAT

HOW FAR DOES A GIRL HAVE TO GO TO UNTANGLE HER TINGLE?

EASTMANCOLOR Ⓧ ADULTS ONLY

CHAPTER 3

PORNO CHIC

1963 to 1973

. . . .

America is deep into its Age of Porn. The old narrow Puritanism is passing, and few mourn it. But the feeling of relief is mixed with growing unease and doubt: How will the current avalanche of porn change America? Many who oppose censorship now wonder if the mounting taste for porn is a symptom of decay, of corrosive boredom, of withdrawal from social concern for obsessive personal pleasures. Even those who argue that it is not harmful to the user, and that people ought to be free to do what they please in private, have begun to fear that the porn plague is in fact invading the privacy of those who want no part of it.

TIME MAGAZINE, 1976

Perhaps the greatest social satirist of the mid-1960s was a Harvard-trained mathematics professor turned edgy cabaret singer. With a sharp eye for hypocrisy and blessed with a wicked wit, Tom Lehrer sang about pollution, Vatican II, nuclear war, and civil rights. On his 1965 album, *That Was the Year That Was*, the sardonic singer added yet another cause to his repertoire: obscenity. That is, "I'm for it." As the audience's laughter diminished, he explained that while his cause was championed on the basis of freedom of speech, "we know what's really involved: dirty books are fun."

Lehrer had seized upon an issue that would roil opinions throughout the next two decades. Along with civil rights, anti-war protests, women's liberation, and burgeoning environmentalism, the nation would debate obscenity. What exactly constitutes obscenity? And what could be done about it? "Obviously, few issues trigger [a] more intense and violent response," declared Robert Taylor in 1969 in the *Boston Globe*. "Those who live by the Puritan Ethic tend to regard the 'New' Morality as the Old Degeneracy."

Understanding the social forces that led to Boston's 1974 establishment of an official zone for adult entertainment requires an examination of how the country's sexual norms were shifting. Dirty books, dirty movies, and dirty dancing were fun, but they were also symbolic of a counter-culture rebellion and middle finger to middle-American morality.

Traditionally, Boston was the haven of the prim and proper, the ghosts of the Puritans flitting in the background to ensure decorum. For nearly eighty years, the Watch and Ward Society—the group that made "Banned in Boston" a label of dubious distinction—sought to keep immoral books and plays out of sight from innocent eyes. This included novels like *An American Tragedy* by Theodore Dreiser and Lillian Hellman's play, *The Children's Hour*.

By the late 1950s, the Watch and Ward Society had fallen from favor, changed its name and focus, and was no longer a protective powerhouse. But Boston still had a city censor: Richard Sinnott. Sinnott's actual title was chief of licensing, but both Sinnott and the press preferred "city censor." A former Associated Press reporter, Sinnott served as press secretary to Mayor John Collins from 1960 to 1967. He was also the chief of the city's licensing division from 1955 until 1982. Holding sway over permits for entertainment venues, he reviewed movies, rock concerts, and other touring shows to determine if the productions met city standards. The zeal with which he tried to prevent what he deemed obscene in plays and movies was well known: his most infamous act was attempting to cut lines from Edward Albee's tour de force, *Who's Afraid of Virginia Woolf?*, which he considered simultaneously brilliant and blasphemous.

Sinnott also served as the city's official greeter. When Jimmy Durante came to Boston for a show, the vaudevillian shook Sinnott's hand, asking, "Are you here to greet me or ban me?" On Mondays, when the new shows came to town, Sinnott would leave his third-floor office in Old City Hall and stroll to the Old Howard Theater and then the Casino in Scollay Square. According to the *Boston Globe*, "he would take his customary seat backstage, so he could view the new shows without being seen by the audience, while he made sure the pasties and G-strings were where they ought to be."

While his name invariably produced a chuckle—Sin Not—the man dubbed "the world's best party pooper" was actually a jaunty Irishman who chain-smoked, liked his bourbon, and was known to use a salty word or two. When burlesque queen Ann Corio died in 1999, he wrote a gushing tribute to her in the *Boston Globe*: "I never met a performer who took her profession more seriously." Nonetheless, Sinnott's sway over Boston's theatrical scene was indisputable, though not always predictable. His seal of disapproval on a theater marquee would either kill a show or ensure its success, all but guaranteeing that curious patrons flocked to see it.

Richard Sinnott, while serving as press secretary for Mayor Collins, standing behind Mary Collins. Courtesy City of Boston.

A Supreme Court precedent set by the 1957 case *Roth v. United States* largely governed Sinnott's decisions, as well as those made by similar officials in other municipalities. The case attempted to define obscenity, which was not protected by the First Amendment. The six-to-three ruling established obscenity as something that "as a whole, appealed to an average person's prurient interest in sex." Obscenity affronted contemporary community standards and/or was without redeeming social value and could therefore be banned. This was, however, an illusive standard. Supreme Court Justice Potter Stewart struggled with the definition of pornography in his concurrence to the 1964 case *Jacobellis v. Ohio*, which ruled that Ohio could not ban as obscene the movie *The Lovers* by Louis Malle. Stewart said he could not attempt to define hardcore obscenity, "but I know it when I see it, and the motion picture involved in this case is not that."

Mr. Sin Not may have thought he knew it when he saw it, but he was powerless against the cultural earthquakes of the late 1960s and early 1970s—the changing norms regarding women's rights, homosexuality, adultery, and even marriage itself. In the mod, mini-skirted, swinging sixties, what was obscene? Surely not *An American Tragedy*. What about *Lady Chatterley's Lover*, the erotic 1928 novel by D.H. Lawrence, which could not be published openly in the United Kingdom until 1960? What about the more explicit *Tropic of Cancer* by Henry Miller? Its publication by Grove Press in 1961 set off a slew of obscenity lawsuits. In 1964, the Supreme Court overturned the state court's ruling of obscenity and declared the book a non-obscene work of literature. It was one step forward for Henry Miller, but a giant leap for the sexual revolution.

What about *Playboy*, founded in 1953 by the granddaddy of sophisticated smut, Hugh Hefner? *Playboy* published works by major literary figures alongside nude photos of women Hefner described as representing the girl next door. Was this obscene or edgy? How about the more explicit *Oui* or *Penthouse* magazines and their nasty cousin, *Screw*, a tabloid launched in 1968 that promised to "uncover the entire world of sex"? *Screw* publisher Al Goldstein, dubbed "the raunch king," announced that pornography was becoming "part of the mainstream of American life."

Carnality was not exclusive to men. In 1971, ex-prostitute Xavier Hollander published her memoir, *The Happy Hooker: My Own Story* and went on to author "Call Me Madam," an advice column for *Penthouse*. In 1973, a young poet published an explicit novel that mirrored Henry Miller in its frank descriptions of sex: Erica Jong and *Fear of Flying* became a sensation, showing that girls could be as randy as the boys, and featuring something called the "zipless fuck."

Nudity was popping up in mainstream movies, and cultural attitudes toward erotic films were also changing. Poorly made stag movies had long been a staple of bachelor parties, and many theaters also showed "skin flicks" or softcore sex films with simulated sex and calculated bits of exposed bodies. The 1960s saw increasingly sophisticated erotic movies, as well as titillating trash like 1968's *Barbarella*, starring Jane Fonda. The Swedish sensation, *I am Curious (Yellow)* mesmerized audiences in the United States, even though the film was seized in Boston on May 10, 1969, by Suffolk County District Attorney Garrett H. Byrne. A legendary prosecutor, a player in Boston politics since the 1940s, and the Boston district attorney since 1952, Byrne had a personal dislike for the enterprises of the Combat Zone. *Yellow* pales, however, beside the explicit, hardcore feature-length movies that began to be released in 1972, including *Deep Throat*, starring Linda Lovelace, *Behind the Green Door* with Marilyn Chambers, and *The Devil in Miss Jones*. With production values higher than those grainy stag films, a semblance of a plot, and close-ups of explicit sex acts, these movies pushed the limits of obscenity to edges hitherto never approached.

Moreover, *Deep Throat* and *The Devil In Miss Jones* enticed a mainstream audience to brave the stigma of going to a skin flick. Movie critic Roger Ebert reviewed *Deep Throat*, writing, "A year or two earlier, porn audiences darted furtively into shabby little theaters on the wrong side of town; now they lined up for *Deep Throat* and talked cheerfully to news cameras about wanting to see it because, well, everybody else seemed to be going." He added, "This is the first stag film to see with a date." The film grossed a fantastic six hundred million dollars, according to Ebert. Johnny Carson and Bob Hope would crack jokes about *Deep Throat*, and *Washington Post* reporter Bob Woodward dubbed one of his Watergate sources Deep Throat.

"This was the time of porno chic. People who would never think of going to the movie houses that cater to the men in the overcoats would see these movies in regular theaters: 'Let's go see this,' giggle, giggle," recalls Boston-area movie booker George J. Mansour, now eighty-two. "It took twenty minutes to get to the screwing scene instead of the first ten minutes." An openly gay man who could not get into college because of his sexual orientation, Mansour began working as a movie booker and was hired by Hallmark, a Boston-based distribution company that focused on low-budget action, horror, and pornography. Movies like *The Devil in Miss Jones*, and later, *Debbie Does Dallas*, were hugely profitable as they were often booked in non-X-rated theaters, he said.

Linda Lovelace, Marilyn Chambers, and Harry Reems became porn superstars. Some even called the early 1970s "the Golden Age of Porn."

Courtesy *Boston Phoenix* archives.

Major media began to review more ambitious softcore and hardcore movies, and according to *Time,* by early 1976, about 780 American theaters routinely showed X-rated movies fifty-two weeks a year.

"There was something exciting about pornography," Norman Mailer said in the documentary *Inside Deep Throat.* "It lived in some mid-world between crime and art. And it was adventurous." Pornographic films were anti-establishment, a continuum of the mentality that sent people into the streets to protest the Vietnam War, Mansour said. No one was more anti-establishment than the deliberately filthy, low-budget filmmaker John Waters, who created a taste for the grotesque with his subversive films like *Mondo Trash* (1969), *Multiple Maniacs* (1970), and the "breakthrough" tour de trash, *Pink Flamingos* (1972). After earning cult status, Waters went on to a successful and more mainstream career.

Hollywood rating codes had to be revised. When first released in 1969, *Midnight Cowboy,* starring John Voight and Dustin Hoffman, sported an X rating. It went on to win three Academy Awards and was the first X-rated film to win best picture. In 1972's X-rated *Last Tango in Paris*, Marlon Brando violated any number of sexual taboos, but today the film is considered a landmark in cinema history. And thus, the XXX rating was born.

There was an implicit stamp, not of approval, but of vague, lukewarm acceptance from the 1970 President's Commission on Obscenity and Pornography, headed by former Illinois Governor Otto Kerner. The commission concluded that pornography was not particularly linked to antisocial behavior and was not a significant cause of sexual crime. These findings were later contradicted in a second presidential commission in 1986 headed by then Attorney General Edwin Meese, which determined that pornography was harmful.

Still, you didn't have to be City Censor Sinnott to know there was a huge difference between *Last Tango* and *Deep Throat*. But the nation's struggle to define obscenity continued. In 1973, the Supreme Court came up with an answer that helped pave the way for the designation of an adult entertainment zone in Boston.

In 1971, mail-order businessman Marvin Miller was convicted by the state of California for mailing illustrated brochures for his pornographic books and films that featured explicit adult material. The case was appealed to the Supreme Court. In a five-to-three decision, written by Chief Justice Warren Burger and released in 1973, the court imposed a new three-part test to determine what was obscene. The basic guidelines, Burger wrote, were: (1) whether "the average person, applying contemporary community standards" would find that the work, taken as a whole, appeals to the prurient interest; (2) whether the work depicts or describes, in a patently offensive way, sexual conduct specifically defined by the applicable state law; and (3) whether the work, taken as a whole, lacks serious literary, artistic, political, or scientific value. This "Miller Test" remains the legal standard for obscenity today, although more stringent criterion has been imposed for child pornography.

The Supreme Court did not eliminate prosecution for obscenity. However, adult entertainment—that is, material for persons over twenty-one years old—was permissible under the law if not deemed to be obscene. State supreme courts began tossing out existing obscenity laws as unconstitutional. The Massachusetts law was tested by a number of cases, including *Commonwealth v. Horton*, in which an employee and the owner of a Quincy bookstore were convicted in

The Paperback Gallery promoting its selection of adult books in downtown Boston during the 1960s. Courtesy City of Boston.

May 1972 of possessing and selling obscene and impure magazines. The defendants appealed to the Massachusetts Supreme Judicial Court and argued that the conviction did not satisfy the First Amendment standards described in *Miller v. California*. In April 1974, the Massachusetts court agreed. Concurrently, the court issued rulings on two other cases that involved attempts to show *The Devil in Miss Jones* and other X-rated movies in Boston theaters. The decision struck down three statutes, one dating from 1711, that comprised the state's criminal laws prohibiting "obscene, indecent, and impure" books, shows, and public entertainment. "In one fell swoop, the court eliminated state statutes dealing with obscenity," the *Boston Globe* reported. "Handfuls of magazines and books, once hidden in the back rooms or secreted behind counters, stared boldly from front-of-the-store racks. Pornography is no longer the sleazy, behind-the-locked-doors business that it used to be."

Many Bostonians were apoplectic, including Boston Police Deputy Superintendent John Doyle, who declared, "Massachusetts has the potential of becoming a mecca of pornography. In the near future we may see live sex shows, bestiality in the movies, and any number of other things. The floodgates of pornography are about to open…"

Boston officials were not alone in feeling under siege by porn merchants. Municipal officers in Detroit and New York City were also struggling with the now wide open floodgates. Interestingly, Detroit opted for the strategy of dispersal: requiring that no sex business could be established within one thousand feet of another. Boston went in a different direction.

Because of the Miller decision, Boston could not close bookstores, movie theaters, or strip clubs on purely moral or nuisance grounds. The Supreme Court's interpretation of the First Amendment meant that adult businesses could be controlled and regulated if they were allowed *somewhere*, but not banned outright. Zoning could not be used to ban all adult business, according to the BRA's Paul McCann. However, "Zoning *can* prohibit them if there is a designated area where they can go."

That was the loophole seized upon by the BRA. You could ban the sleaze here if you allowed it over there. And "there" was the Combat Zone, which was already chock-a-block with dirty bookstores, peep shows, strip clubs, and XXX-rated movie theaters. BRA planners concentrated on what they believed was their only option: containment. They would draw a line around the existing businesses and hold them in, like wild horses in a corral. They saw this solution as a unique fix, possibly even a model for the country. It would, in many respects, be a deal with the devil.

CHAPTER 4

CREATING AN ADULT PLAYGROUND

April to November 1974

....

The zoning didn't create the Combat Zone.
The Combat Zone created the zoning.

BARNEY FRANK, *BOSTON PHOENIX*, 1977

There's good money to be made by taking off your clothes, but there's better money to be made by putting on a good face. Debra Beckerman, a former nightclub dancer turned public relations professional, who touted degrees from Julliard and the Boston Conservatory, learned this in the early 1970s when she became the official spokesperson for the Combat Zone. An exotic beauty with long, dark hair framing an oval face, Beckerman, like all good PR flacks, had one mission: to ensure that her clients were seen in a positive light. In this case, the clients in question were Boston's merchants of smut.

Gossip circulated about Beckerman, some of which—according to her—was started by the vice squad in Boston. "There were rumors going around that I was just a very intelligent stripper who got fat, but could talk. The police had a rumor that I was the daughter of a famous Mafioso ... when they found out I was just a poor little converted Jew who was the PR director at Kennedy Hospital it killed 'em." In reality, Beckerman hailed from Waterville, Maine. According to some reports, she ran away to Las Vegas at the age of seventeen and worked as a Playboy bunny. When she returned to New England in her late twenties, Beckerman took a job as director of public relations for the Kennedy Memorial Hospital in Brighton.

Beckerman claims it was her boyfriend, Jack Kelly, who took her to her first Boston strip club in 1973. Kelly was a popular and well-regarded (if sensation-inclined) investigative reporter for Channel 7, often tasked with reporting on the Zone. "Jack introduced me to some people, and I concluded that the place was not so bad. I wasn't mugged or accosted on the street, and the show featured attractive young women in beautiful costumes—not a bunch of old ladies with bad bodies doing obscene things as I had expected," she told the *Boston Phoenix*.

One of the people Beckerman met was Christie L. "Teddy" Venios, an underworld figure with a number of investments in Combat Zone businesses, including the Two O'Clock Lounge. Teddy and his brothers, Arthur and Louis Venios, hailed from Woburn, Massachusetts, and had long rap sheets, that included arrests and sentences for fraud, swindles, illegal gambling, and schemes to distribute obscene material. Venios, known on the street as Teddy Venus, was among the most prominent Combat Zone operators with alleged links to organized crime. With his short, squat stature and pug nose, Teddy Venus looked the part. But Beckerman wasn't deterred by his unsavory repute. "Your streets are dirty, your reputation is lousy," she told him. "What you people need is a good PR person. I can help you improve your image." Teddy Venus was impressed; he hired Beckerman, giving her an office in the Capri Cinema, a porn theater on Washington Street. Her mandate was to make the X-rated businesses of the Zone more palatable to the public. She would give the Zone some tone and stature without disguising its basic character.

Beckerman took her job seriously, becoming the attractive, professional public face of Boston's sex industry. She met with city officials, attended community meetings, and was always ready to give a quote to the press. In April 1974, when the Massachusetts Supreme Judicial Court tossed out the Commonwealth's obscenity statutes, Beckerman led the cheering squad, telling the *Globe*, "The laws we had were Victorian and the people enforcing them were creeps who want to keep even *Playboy* off the newsstands. We believe you can draw a line somewhere, but it has to be open-minded enough for this day and age."

Beckerman wanted to help draw that line. And so, this sharp spokeswoman for smut became allies with the agency charged with ushering in New Boston.

◆

On May 30, 1970, a $300 million redevelopment and urban renewal initiative was announced for Park Square. Proposed by Mortimer Zuckerman, the mammoth Park Plaza Project called for five skyscrapers to be built on a thirty-five-acre parcel, replacing the derelict and seedy Park Square. This development, had it happened, would have involved demolishing low-income neighborhoods, including razing portions of the Combat Zone as well as the strip clubs that had opened on Boylston Street. The wrecking ball almost took care of the Combat Zone at this point, but despite the city's support for the project, the public vehemently opposed it as too massive for the area. After many debates and various modifications, the project was eventually abandoned, and city officials looked for other ways to rejuvenate and improve Boston's broken downtown. Robert T. Kenney, who took over as the BRA's director in 1971, and Mayor White focused their sights on the Combat Zone.

Kenney, who had been running the city's Public Facilities Department, was a contrast to the charismatic Ed Logue. A talented, self-effacing manager, Kenney was willing to tackle complicated projects with a cool, non-political eye. Over the next six years, Kenney led the BRA in a multitude of revitalization efforts like the South Cove Project, which included development in Chinatown, Park Square, and nearby medical complexes, as well as the Combat Zone. Under Kenney, the BRA revitalized the Faneuil Hall Marketplace, a project deemed as successful as the West End was a failure.

But what to do with the Combat Zone? Various ideas were floated. Could the shops and theaters be closed down without the smut spreading to other areas of the city? Or shipped out to a Boston Harbor island to create a "wild sort of Coney Island?" The BRA opted for containment; that is, to make the Combat Zone the only place in the city where sex businesses could officially operate, as long as they did not engage in prostitution or other illegal activities. Businesses outside the Zone would not be granted necessary licenses to run strip joints, X-rated movie theaters, or bookstores. Adult enterprises in Park Square would be allowed to continue under "grandfather" rules, but once they closed, no other adult enterprise could open.

But the BRA intended to do more than "zone and be damned." The authority's architects and planners worked with Combat Zone businesses to improve signage, lighting, and street-level appearances. The goal was to make the area cleaner and safer and thus improve the downtown in general.

The district certainly needed a facelift. The BRA made plans to establish a small urban park at the corner of Washington and Boylston to be called Liberty Tree Park. Kenney even suggested changing the name of the Combat Zone to "Liberty Tree" to help polish its image. "We have picked Liberty Tree but it is only a suggestion. If that name doesn't catch on, maybe we could have a contest," Kenney told the *Boston Herald*. Beckerman proposed calling the area the "Erogenous Zone."

Another factor driving the BRA toward containment was this dirty little secret about the Combat Zone: it was a lucrative tourist attraction. As a 1974 BRA report would acknowledge, "Conventioneers with money won't come to Boston without the Zone..." Strip clubs were left off official itineraries, but their existence certainly influenced convention planners. While the conventioneers' wives were shopping on Newbury Street or walking the Freedom Trail, the boys would hit the clubs on Washington Street. David Waller, who was a nineteen-year-old doorman at the Parker House hotel on School Street, remembers the men who approached him in whispers, "Where can a guy get some action?" He would tell them, "Just walk to the end of the block and turn right, you'll know it when you get there." This was worth a twenty-dollar tip.

"I'd like to see what would happen to Boston's convention business if we weren't here," one bookstore owner put it bluntly. The BRA was also painfully aware that investment throughout downtown Boston was moribund. Say what you will about the strip clubs and stores, they made money. "Even as the Zone was represented by most [even those who worked there or frequented it] as morally problematic and dirty, it was also seen as economically viable, pumping money into the city by attracting suburbanites and conventioneers," wrote Eric Schaefer and Eithne Johnson in "Quarantined! A Case Study of Boston's Combat Zone," a chapter of the book *Hop on Pop: The Politics and Pleasures of Popular Culture.* "The zone was a hybrid space, a threatening and thrilling urban carnival."

Daniel J. Ahern, the influential executive director of the Back Bay Federation for Community Development, wrote to the BRA in 1973: "We would be unwise to assume that all of the eighteen million visitors will be clean-minded mid-Americans who will spend their daytimes tramping the Freedom Trail and then, after a New England boiled dinner, bed down at an early hour … We must recognize that the Bicentennial hordes will contain a fair number of swingers who will be looking for night life in the city. … nightclubs, topless restaurants, porno movies, and the other kinds of entertainment which they associate with big-city life at its very best."

Both Mayor White and his top cop favored creating an adult entertainment district. In 1972, White went outside the circle of Boston's police community and hired Robert diGrazia, a reform-minded cop, as the city's new police commissioner. Ambitious and controversial, diGrazia shook things up in the department; not only did he support the creation of the Zone, he ended the practice of allowing its bars to hire police details, effectively pulling the cops out of the Zone. That left many rank-and-file police officers, including those on the vice squad, aghast. As one detective put it: "the imbeciles, the morons … knew nothing of what they were doing." While politicians, including then state representative Barney Frank, praised diGrazia for his innovations, veteran cops like Ed McNelley considered him "a snake oil salesman."

In April 1974, the BRA circulated a draft plan for establishing a five-and-a-half-acre site, bisected by lower Washington Street, as an "adult entertainment district." The city that made "Banned in Boston" a rallying cry now proposed to set up a sanctioned district for strip clubs, nude dancing, X-rated movies, smutty books, peep shows, sex-toy shops, and all manner of pornography.

The cover of the BRA's 1974 Adult Entertainment District Study features a saucy caricature of what a bunch of Yankees might look like on their way to an orgy. The lively, crowded street is filled with sailors, scantily clad women, and a man with a Filene's bag amidst gaudy signs hawking "Strippers and Dancers," "All girl show," and "Gay 'n Frisky." The "Twinx Cinema" is showing *Deep Throat*. Chesty Morgan has her name in lights. Under the street signs of Washington and Essex, there's a sign warning "No Gravestone Rubbing," a nod to the notices posted in Boston's historic graveyards. Right over the address of 103 Washington is a sly wink to the Combat Zone's own PR gal, Debra Beckerman. The building is called "Beckerman Arms." Such a cover for an official city government study will likely never be seen again, underscoring the "if you can't beat them, join them" sort of joie de vivre.

The BRA made this clear: The city would not give any official sanction or approval to "illegal or immoral" activity. Rather, the BRA (and the city by default) would chart a course "that will enhance the physical and economic well-being of the city and will not interfere with the constitutional privileges of those who wish to participate in adult entertainment activities." Judging from the cover of the Adult Entertainment District Study, the Zone, which had become sleazier than anything imagined in Scollay Square, would be Disneyfied.

In May 1974, the amendment to Boston's zoning code was formally proposed; the issue was debated over the subsequent summer and into the fall. While *Boston Herald* columnist Cornelius Timilty argued that "a small bomb be dropped on the Combat Zone," the *Boston Globe* supported the amendment, opining, "Permitting [adult entertainment] in one area is not only a refreshingly frank acknowledgment of reality, but it also helps to ensure that the new zoning amendment could sustain a court challenge that the city was discriminating against lawful business activity." Even famed conservative William F. Buckley supported the concept of an official red-light zone, asserting "The Boston experiment should be indulged. The anti-obscenity people should keep quiet about it." The BRA also argued that the ancillary benefit of a designated zone was that it also allowed those who wished to avoid such activities to steer clear. (Of course,

Courtesy City of Boston.

those who lived in Chinatown or worked in the nearby hospitals and buildings might have had something to say about that.) Paul McCann believes to this day that the city, given the *Miller v. California* ruling, had few options. The Combat Zone "was already there," he said. "The zoning was to control it."

At that time, the average Bostonian probably wasn't paying much attention to the actions of the city's zoning board. In June of 1974, Federal District Court Judge W. Arthur Garrity ruled that the city's schools were deliberately segregated. He ordered that white and black students be bused to schools outside their neighborhoods to achieve education equality for all. South Boston erupted in dissent, and demonstrators pelted school buses of black children with stones. Police were called to quell protests and Boston became a symbol of the racial divide in America. The school busing crisis dominated the media headlines and the city feared a race war would break out in the streets. All over the city and its greater metropolitan area, citizens were organizing for or against bussing. Opponents of the proposed adult entertainment district lacked this organized drive. In September, the BRA faced the last challenge: convincing the Boston Zoning Commission that Boston needed its own officially sanctioned sexual playground.

◆

Just after half past three on September 11, 1974, one of Boston's most dynamic young legislators rose to address the Boston Zoning Commission. He had thick glasses and a round face, and during his tenure as an aide to Mayor White, he was known for padding around City Hall in his stocking feet. Nonetheless, he was skilled in the Hub's favorite blood sport: politics. A graduate of Harvard Law School, he was shrewd, a master of facts, and armed with a cutting wit. He represented his Back Bay constituency in the Massachusetts legislature with a ward politician's tenacity coupled with his support of liberal, even libertarian, issues. While seemingly fearless, the young man harbored a personal secret that he would not publically reveal for another thirteen years.

On that day, however, he spoke bluntly about sex. "The fact is there always has been and always will be commercial sex-type activities in the heart of a major metropolitan center," he told the members of the zoning commission in room 921 of Boston City Hall. "Realistically we are probably a lot closer to curing cancer than we are socially to curing commercially oriented sexual activity."

State Representative Barney Frank was on a roll, explaining how the BRA's proposed amendment to create an adult entertainment district in the heart of downtown Boston was sensible, realistic, and well-thought-out. "It seemed to me that the authority here has shown an unusual amount of common sense for a government agency of any type," he asserted.

Commissioner Alfred Gross, representing the Master Builders Association of Boston, was not buying it. "What you are asking our board here to do is to actually perpetuate an area of vice!" he said.

"No sir," Frank replied. "I'm not asking you to perpetuate it. I am asking you to prevent its spread."

Containment? Or sowing vice? These were the questions the zoning commission considered with Item 44-165, the second of three items scheduled for hearings that day. BRA officials came prepared with documents and maps laying out the exact location for this new adult entertainment zone, down to the foot. The proposed zoning language also allowed for flashing and moving lights, which were banned elsewhere in Boston. The minutes of that meeting hashed out the arguments for and against the Zone—arguments that were glossed over by the media at the time, which was focused on the busing issue.

"The program that we propose is bold and controversial, but it's also rational and forward-looking," Kenney told the commissioners. Allston, Brighton, Back Bay, Beacon Hill, Bay Village, and Chinatown "are the areas of the city that are threatened by the uncontrolled spread of the adult entertainment uses in addition to the downtown commercial section. That is why we decided that, rather than continue the policy of turning our back on adult entertainment uses, we would face the issue and take the steps to protect the residential neighborhoods of the city."

"We are not condoning illegal activities. That is a matter for the courts, the legislature, and the police department, but even under the new laws of obscenity, uncontrolled spread of these uses throughout the city creates a blighting effect on the residential neighborhoods. We think it's about time to face the issue and to try to contain it." You can't, he stressed, change human nature with a wrecking ball.

Other supporters added their voices to Kenney's, including Joseph M. Smith, chairman of the Allston Civic Association, Stuart Robbins, Little City Hall Member for Beacon Hill, Neal Widett of the Beacon Hill Civic Association, and Daniel J. Ahern.

In light of what would follow, it is surprising that Peter Chan, field representative of Chinatown's Little City Hall, spoke in support of the amendment. Indeed, Chan recalls that moment with mixed emotions. His position was influenced by Chinatown's losing battles with the city during the 1950s and early 1960s, which he referenced in his remarks. Compared to the heavy-handed Central Artery project, the adult entertainment district proposal seemed almost neighborhood friendly. While supporters like Ahern and Frank were operating out of NIMBY—Not In My Back Yard—concerns, Chinatown residents were already coping with the strip clubs, movies, and bookstores in their front yards. The BRA had reassured the Chinese community that the amendment would lead to the containment of adult entertainment. "We like to take these words literally and seriously," Chan said. "Because of our faith and optimism in the government process, I sincerely recommend the proposed amendment." Decades later, Chan acknowledged in an interview that the zoning amendment was "not the best idea but not totally a bad idea. It just seemed the best option at the time."

Debra Beckerman, the only female to testify at the hearing, also spoke in favor of the amendment.

Then opponents were heard. They did not hold back. Some Chinatown residents—in a preview of what was to come—fiercely opposed the Zone. In a written statement to the commission, May-Ling Tong, another Chinatown leader, complained that the BRA considered it worthwhile to contain the Combat Zone "to protect all other Boston neighborhoods . . . [but] it seems to have forgotten that there is a very neglected community and residential area bordering the Combat Zone."

The comments of George McLaughlin, representing the Sack Theater chain (which included the Saxon Theater, Gary Theater, and Savoy) dripped with vitriol. That morning, a Sack Theater official had described the Combat Zone to the *Boston Herald* as "Satan's Playground," and McLaughlin upped the ante. "This is an area in which every form of vice known to man thrives," McLaughlin said.

"This is an area to be devoted to prostitutes, pimps, pornographers, pushers, and perverts," he declared. "It's a 'p' zone, not an 'e' zone. ... By God, one thing the city of Boston has always had is character until I hear somebody like Barney Frank talking and then I am convinced that there is damn little character in the city of Boston."

McLaughlin, however, had another agenda: Sack management believed that a legitimate adult entertainment district would steal customers from its theaters. Indeed, the Sack was quick to rant and rave about the alleged debauchery going on in the Combat Zone but was rather silent about the explicit sex and violence in some of its R-rated features like *The Godfather* and *Death Wish*, writes Salvatore M. Giorlandino in his dissertation on the origin, development, and decline of the Combat Zone. In fact, the Sack once sought to show *Deep Throat* at one of its theaters, and the previous year, the Sack had fought a Danvers, Massachusetts selectmen restriction on showing adult films at its new four-theater complex off of Route 128. Still, McLaughlin railed like a fire-and-brimstone preacher at the zoning commissioners: "Almighty God made man, and since man is imperfect and prone to sin, let's keep all his sins in one spot in the town. Well, you know that is just about as crazy as anything can possibly be."

William F. Chouinard of the Boston Chamber of Commerce warned of a double standard in promoting the best use of the land downtown: why should adult entertainment, not considered a sound business, be allowed to exist in one area and not in another? Opponents representing Don Bosco Technical High School voiced safety concerns, as did Edward Erlich, representing the Tufts-New England Medical Center. "We fear this kind of redevelopment will establish a rotten core in the city," he said.

Two months later, on November 14, 1974, the zoning board approved the amendment. Just four days after that, the Combat Zone made national headlines in a totally unanticipated fashion.

Arkansas Congressman Wilbur Mills on stage with Annabella Battistella, also known as the Argentine Firecracker.

THE POLITICIAN AND THE FOXE

October to November 1974

· ·

Instead of acting like a hypocrite, the chairman came to Boston and went directly to Fanne Foxe's cloakroom at the Pilgrim Theater. No secret liaisons in out of the way motel rooms for him. His feelings have been laid bare for the public at large to see and hear. If monogamy were a qualification for membership in Congress, there would never be a quorum.

MIKE BARNICLE, *BOSTON GLOBE*, DECEMBER 4, 1974

In a city of powerful men, Arkansas Congressman Wilbur Mills was among the most formidable. "I never vote against God, motherhood, or Wilbur Mills," a colleague once said. As chairman of the House Ways and Means Committee in the 1970s, the Democratic representative was a canny, calculating player in the mythical smoke-filled rooms where bills were brought to fruition, deals were brokered, or legislative dreams scuttled. His craggy face graced the cover of *Time* magazine in 1963, and he even flirted with a presidential run in 1972.

In the fall of 1974, as Boston's officials debated the creation of the AED, the sixty-five-year-old Mills was at the peak of his power. He had been a lawmaker for thirty-six years and had been married to his loyal wife, Polly, for four decades. All of Washington knew that Mills was a good ol' boy, a hard drinker with an eye for the ladies, traits that were not, in those days, a political career buster. His clout in Washington was absolute, until an evening in the Combat Zone a mere four days after Boston's zoning commissioner approved the AED.

The events leading to that night began weeks earlier in the wee hours of October 9, 1974, in Washington, DC, when Mills was in a car stopped by police for erratic driving. One of the car's passengers, a dark-haired, statuesque thirty-eight-year-old named Annabella Battistella, leaped out of the vehicle and into the Tidal Basin, a small estuary of the Potomac River. She had to be fished out by the authorities. When police refused to let Mills drive her home, he retorted, "I'm a congressman and I'll have you demoted." Turns out Mrs. Battistella was a stripper who performed under the name of Fanne Foxe at a club called the Silver Slipper. A native of a small town outside of Buenos Aires, her saucy act had earned her the name of the "Argentine Firecracker."

Those were the days when the press would simply look the other way when a congressman got frisky. But the Firecracker's Tidal Basin plunge was just too juicy to ignore, and the national media reveled in accounts of the stripper and the congressmen.

Both Mills and Battistella insisted they were just close friends; Mills huffed to reporters he was helping Mrs. Battistella's career just as he would for any constituent in need. In fact, the Mills and the Battistellas, Eduardo and Annabella, lived in the same Arlington, Virginia, apartment complex. Although Annabella backed up Mills' story, Mills' re-election in November 1974 was not, as per usual, a foregone conclusion. Still, his Arkansas constituency forgave their good ol' boy, and he was re-elected by a comfortable margin.

Life was also good to Annabella Battistella. Performing as Fanne Foxe, she greatly enjoyed her fifteen minutes. Notoriety never hurts a stripper's career and she now had plenty. After the events, she was now known as the "Washington Tidal Basin Bombshell," and Foxe was suddenly in huge demand. All the strip clubs were hot to book her, including the Pilgrim Theater in Boston's Combat Zone.

Once a legitimate theater with a long and illustrious history, the Pilgrim Theater now resembled a showgirl past her prime. It opened in May 1912 as Gordon's Olympia, featuring live plays, vaudeville, and eventually talking movies. By the 1950s, the theater, now called the Pilgrim, screened mainly movies, and by the 1960s, most of them were naughty: *Sexus, The Garden of Eden, Dr. Sex, Kipling's Women,* and *A Bawdy Tale of a Naughty Doctor.*

In the 1970s, the Pilgrim was taken over by Joe Savino, a former candy seller for the Old Howard in Scollay Square. A would-be entertainment entrepreneur, Savino decided in 1973 that Boston was ready for a return to burlesque, or "burlesk" as he spelled it. What he had in mind was not just the kind of bare-it-all strippers like those at the Two O'Clock. No, Savino wanted the style and flair of striptease stars like Tempest Storm, Chesty Morgan, and Blaze Starr. Savino poured money into upgrading the old Pilgrim from X-rated porn to G-string performances by May of 1973. A *Globe* theater critic quipped it was "like shifting from a boilermaker to a high ball."

Savino booked Chesty Morgan, the blonde with a seventy-plus-inch bust. Chesty Morgan's bosom won her notoriety far beyond her abilities. She wore one hundred dollar brassieres that were custom-made with size double-P cups. She was known for walking onto the stage with two small men in front of her, each carrying a breast. For Savino, however, Chesty was a godsend, packing the house. By October 1974, Savino wanted to book the nation's most famous stripper: Fanne Foxe. He was willing to pay whatever it took. In this case, three thousand dollars a week.

Fanne Foxe's Boston stint began on November 18, 1974, with a press conference at the 57 Restaurant in Park Square. The ink was still wet on the zoning commission's amendment that created the adult entertainment district. Foxe, dressed in a tight white turtleneck sweater and slacks, talked as her handlers popped open champagne for reporters. In the room was City Censor Richard Sinnott and *Boston Globe* columnist Jeremiah V. Murphy, who was having a very good time. Murphy noted that Fanne "seemed a little brighter than most strippers." (One wonders how he knew this.)

Foxe filled the seats at the Pilgrim for two weeks. Everyone wanted to see the stripper who had nearly derailed a congressman's career. On the night of November 30, Foxe came on stage in a bra and dark panties—that gave the impression she had even less than she did—and a gossamer negligee with ruffs of dark feathers at the sleeves. She startled her audience with an announcement. "I'd like you to meet

Fanne Fox, enjoying her fifteen minutes of fame.
Courtesy *Boston Herald*.

somebody," she said, and then turned and called into the wings. "Mr. Mills, Mr. Mills! Where are you?"

A grinning Wilbur Mills staggered on stage in a suit and tie, his gray hair slicked back. He grasped Foxe's hand, letting the dark feathers caress his wrist like the touch of doom. They quipped, they kissed, and he left as the audience slowly realized they had just witnessed a political suicide in action. Someone snapped a photo of a sloshed congressman and his "protégé" on the stage of a strip club. It appeared the next day in a Boston newspaper.

That was it for Mills' political career. He tried to explain he was simply helping Foxe's career, that she was better than Gypsy Rose Lee. But the good ol' boy had gone too far. In December, Mills announced he would resign as chairman of the House Ways and Means Committee. He checked himself into the Naval Medical Center in Bethesda, Maryland, admitted to a severe drinking problem, and joined Alcoholics Anonymous. He did not run for re-election in 1976. He died in 1992 at the age of eighty-two.

Foxe, who always called her former patron "Mr. Mills," managed to ride her notoriety for a few more years. She continued to strip, but on December 12, 1974, she was arrested at a topless bar in Casselberry, Florida, charged with dancing bottomless. With the help of Yvonne Dunleavy, who co-wrote *The Happy Hooker,* she authored *The Stripper and the Congressman*, in which she claimed that she and Mills were in love, but his wife wouldn't grant a divorce. Fanne eventually faded from the national stage, a footnote in the annals of politicians behaving badly.

Not even Foxe could revive the glory days of burlesque. On May 30, 1975, George McKinnon of the *Globe* reported with relish that burlesque at the Pilgrim was grinding to a halt. The theater would end its days as an X-rated movie house and a hook-up place for gay men. It continued to produce juicy tidbits, including a long circulated but never verified story that a Catholic priest suffered and died from a heart attack while watching a film there. But the Pilgrim will always be remembered for providing a stage for the first in a series of men in high political office who didn't know when to keep their pants zipped.

Lucy Wightman, also known as Princess Cheyenne. Courtesy *Boston Herald*.

CHAPTER 5

GIRLS, GIRLS, GIRLS

....

Like a talented revivalist preacher, Rebel could work her audience into a frenzy. … She began her sermon by strutting to the far end of the runway. The congregation began to sway. "She's so fine." Back down at the fat end of the T-shaped runway, she leaned with her arms outstretched against the black backdrop. "Do it, baby." She tossed her dark hair back, a move that drew a plaintive moan from the audience. … And then she made her first offering: breasts. …

LAURI LEWIN, *NAKED IS THE BEST DISGUISE*

G rowing up as the daughter of a Jewish delicatessen owner, Julie Hurwitz and her mother never missed seeing film versions of popular musicals. As they took their seats in one of Boston's downtown theaters, Julie would be transported to another place and time: the streets of New York in *West Side Story*, rural America in *The Music Man*, or San Francisco's Chinatown in *Flower Drum Song*. When no one was around, Julie played the soundtracks on her parents' record player at home and danced in the living room, imagining herself on stage. In 1962, she and her mom saw the film *Gypsy*, based on the musical inspired by stripper Gypsy Rose Lee. Julie, then a boyish nine-year-old sandwiched between two brothers, was enthralled by Natalie Wood's transformation from shy tomboy to sultry diva.

Julie was a child of the 1960s, rebellious, independent, and spirited. She dabbled in marijuana, briefly ran away to New York City at fifteen, and after graduating Brookline High School in 1971, she ended up on the road with her first love in their converted Tip Top Bread truck. By early 1974, she was back in the Boston area after a failed attempt to live in a teepee in the Colorado Mountains with the boyfriend who took the lyrics "love the one you're with" too literally. Monogamy was considered conservative for those swinging times.

By twenty, Julie was living unhappily in her parents' apartment and struggling to find meaningful employment. She reached back to her childhood for comfort. She put on a record and danced out her frustration, shedding her shirt as she heated up. She caught a glimpse of herself in a mirror, suddenly aware of her striking hourglass figure. She'd heard there were clubs hiring go-go dancers in the Combat Zone. Why not become a dancer like the girls she grew up watching on TV? So early one evening, decked out in her jean skirt and hiking boots, she hopped the T downtown.

She walked into the first strip club she saw: the Mousetrap in Park Square. She cautiously sat down at the bar and quickly noticed she was the only female in the room. In a few minutes, a young woman appeared on the small stage, wearing nothing but a bra, G-string, and negligee. As a jukebox played a popular rock tune, the dancer began to gyrate and shake, twisting and turning with the dexterity of a cobra. This was nothing like go-go dancing, but Julie was intrigued enough to stick around.

After a few of these dancers performed, a live band struck up a tune and an emcee appeared. These girls had only been warm-up acts. The main event was yet to come.

The next dancer wasn't wearing the skimpy three pieces of clothing that the previous ones sported. She strutted out in a shimmering gown that glittered like the night sky. When she started to dance, her arms, legs, and torso moved in syncopation to music—the effect was both seductive and scary. When she shed a piece of clothing, it seemed like an act of freedom.

Julie wanted to run out of the club but was glued to her seat. It felt so electrifying to even be there. Could she actually do this? Everything she did in the privacy of her bedroom was improvised. She didn't know how to be sexy. She didn't even wear makeup. But when the manager appeared out of the darkness and asked her if she wanted a job dancing in one of the early sets, she said sure, why not. Come back tomorrow, he said.

The following day, Julie returned (still in her jean skirt and boots, but this time armed with a male friend as backup) and followed the manager upstairs to the dressing room. It was straight out of *Gypsy*. Wall-to-wall mirrors lit by bare bulbs, half-dressed women with false eyelashes and forty pounds of makeup apiece. The walls were lined with what appeared to be thousands of dollars' worth of custom-made costumes.

The ladies in the dressing room took one look at Julie's boots, skirt, makeup-free face, and unshaven legs and rolled their eyes. They outfitted her in a sparkly bra, a G-string, and negligee. "How do I know when to take them off?" Julie asked the manager. He said, "Well, there are three songs and you have three pieces. As long as you have something off by the end of each song, you're doing fine."

Julie tried to quell a sense of panic. But the thrill of this challenge and the plunge into the unknown pulled at her like the promise of a new kind of high. In her borrowed wardrobe and bare feet, she stepped on stage when the music began, trying to copy the slinky moves of the girls she'd watched the day before. The first song ended and she slipped the negligee from her shoulders. When the second song ended, the bra came off. She waited for the very last note of the last song to remove the G-string, so she wouldn't be naked but for the blink of an eye. It was horrifying. Intoxicating. Amazing. Nasty. Almost against her will, she came back the next night. And the next. And the next.

Under the name Julie Jordan, this girl from Brookline danced in Combat Zone clubs for the next three years. Even after her parents kicked her out. Even as she continued to question herself. It wasn't just the money, although the money was great. Stripping, she recalled, "wasn't a boring sales clerk position or stupid waitress job. It was show business. It was live music. It was these incredible costumes. It was these talented women who had acts. They choreographed their dances. They put a lot of thought into it. It was like walking onto a movie set. It was like being in the world of *Gypsy*."

At least, that's how it first felt to a young Jewish hippie chick fresh from a teepee in the Colorado Mountains.

Men and mobsters owned the businesses of the Combat Zone and the customers were largely male, but women were the Zone's economic engines even if they were not the ones reaping the largest profit. Telling the stories of a few of these dancers is to walk through a minefield of isms: eroticism, sexism, and feminism. Their stories are full of contradictions; they describe life in the Combat Zone as simultaneously exciting and degrading, salacious and humiliating, tragic and comic. And sometimes lucrative.

Dancers had names like Kendra Wilde, Panama Red, Lolita, and Tangerine. Transsexual performers like Onyx and Brittany (allegedly a former US Marine) were popular. Some worked as warm-up acts or so-called go-go dancers. Headliners began their acts dressed for the prom and ended up in their birthday suits. A general striptease lasted four to five songs: the negligee would disappear during the first song, the bra in the second, then the jock—which was something like a thong—in the third. This left the G-string underneath. By the end of the last song, the G-string would be gone, too.

Unlike today's gentlemen's clubs, there were no poles and no lap dances. The acts were well choreographed and occasionally built

©Jerry Berndt Estate.

around edgy stage personas. Machine Gun Kelly would pop out of a coffin, armed with a fake machine gun. Another dancer played a vampire; she sprayed her audience with fake blood. One performer went full S&M with whips and chains. Another woman danced with a boa constrictor; "It doesn't bother me," she told the *New York Times*. "I've been around reptiles all my life." Julie Jordan remembers a performer with a huge champagne glass. "She would climb the ladder and swim around. It was filled with water and she did this whole act in the champagne glass."

Jonathan Tudan, a graduate of Wentworth Institute who wrote a memoir about his time managing a Combat Zone apartment building that was home to strippers, hookers, drug dealers, and musicians (including famed doo-wop singer Little Joe Cook), describes a particularly memorable act: one popular stripper worked her audience into such a frenzy that patrons continued to scream, "Take it off!" even after she was totally nude. So she pulled out her false teeth and tossed them into the crowd.

There was a clear social distinction between hookers on the streets and dancers in the clubs. Did a few dancers go out with customers? Yes. Did more than a few—either under duress or by volition—perform sex acts for men in the dark corners of clubs? Yes. In fact, some of the clubs had designated private rooms where this sort of thing could happen for a fee. Generally speaking, dancers distinguished themselves from the working girls who hung out at Good Time Charlie's on LaGrange Street. An invisible but palatable barrier separated the dancers from the streetwalkers, a barrier of economics and race. "The strippers and prostitutes did not get along as a rule," Tudan writes. "The strippers were from a higher strata than the prostitutes."

Although there were a few successful black dancers, including the esteemed transsexual Onyx, most dancers were white. The standards of beauty, as one former performer noted, were very much Nordic and Eurocentric, whereas a large portion of the Combat Zone's prostitutes were black or Latino. The Naked i's promise of a "Totally Nude College Girl Revue" catered to this kind of class prejudice.

Still, there was more than a bit of truth to the "college girl" label. A number of dancers did indeed work their way through college by dancing in the Zone. Others were mothers, single or married, trying to support their families. Many simply didn't have alternative economic choices. A few, however, came from middle-class or even well-off backgrounds and were fortunate enough to use dancing as a springboard to a life outside the Zone.

One of these was Elizabeth T. Brawner, who was raised in a well-to-do home near Washington, DC. She began to dance at the age of twenty under the name of Kendra Wilde. "I was drawn to it. No one talked me into it," she recalled. She soon developed her persona, dancing to the Sex Pistols and The Clash. "I was the edgiest dancer there," she said. "I pushed the envelope when it came to music. I wasn't conventional at all."

Another was Lauri Umansky, a Jewish girl who spent her youth in the American South and New York City before winding up on her own as a teenager in Boston. A proverbial wild child, she started stripping at the Two O'Clock at age sixteen. The petite blonde also found work at the Naked i. At just over five feet, "I looked about twelve. I looked like a child. I knowingly played on that," she recalled. She chose "Lolita" as her stage name, with the smug satisfaction that club owners knew nothing about Nabokov's famous novel of underage obsession. The money she made put her through college, but the cost was an uneasy bargain with her own feminist tendencies. Under the name Lauri Lewin, she later wrote the memoir, *Naked is the Best Disguise: My Life as a Stripper,* which details some of the more sordid incidents from her dancing days—including forced sex acts and an attack—while describing the heady allure of stripping before a rapt, adoring crowd. She and fellow dancers debated whether their work was sensuous or obscene, she wrote. "We concurred that the female body, graceful and lovely, ought to be admired. Some dancers felt that the floorshow afforded the possibility for healthy admiration."

Perhaps the most storied dancer in the Combat Zone was Princess Cheyenne, who still elicits sighs of pleasure and nostalgia from a generation of Boston-area men who saw her dance in faux Native American splendor at the Naked i. Known as "The Thinking Man's Stripper"—an unforgettable tag line for an exotic dancer—Princess Cheyenne is to the Combat Zone what Gypsy Rose Lee was to burlesque and Carol Doda was to San Francisco's legendary North Beach.

Princess Cheyenne was born Lucy Wightman in 1959 in a tony

suburb of Chicago. By her own account, she was kicked out of a private girls' high school in 1975 for acknowledging that she had smoked pot, and by age seventeen she was crisscrossing the country with a divorced lawyer twice her age. At eighteen, she applied for a job as an exotic dancer at Boston's Pussy Cat Lounge but didn't like the club's practice of allowing men to touch women. The Naked i proved to be a better fit for a girl who insisted that "all she wanted to do was take her clothes off" and dance.

According to various accounts, the Naked i's owners ran a "pretty straight place." Dancers wore long gowns and could only be touched on the shoulder or knee, said Kendra Wilde, adding, "The Naked i was a classy strip joint—if you could call a strip joint classy." The club was far too profitable to risk being shuttered for misconduct. Indeed, one former bartender, Joel A. Feingold, estimated the club's Budweiser sales were second only to Fenway Park's.

It was Naked i's management that created her Princess Cheyenne persona, a role that came with a soft leather skirt trimmed with intricate colorful beadwork and a huge, dramatic headdress adorned with blue feathers and white velvet that rose two feet above her and trailed down to the floor. Princess Cheyenne was soon a headline act. "She actually danced to the music rather than strutted. She put on a show," Lewin wrote in her memoir.

Princess Cheyenne was featured in *People* magazine, in part because of her brief engagement to singer Cat Stevens. She was articulate, often penning articles about

Princess Cheyenne in full dress.
Courtesy *Boston Herald*.

herself. "No local stripper had been paid more or received more publicity," she declared in a *Boston Magazine* article. "I'd become a star with money in the bank and power—if only inside the club. But success was a delicate illusion. I'd given up wanting sex with men. And I was getting bored." She left the Naked i in 1982 to marry a police officer and went back to school to study journalism. Two years later, she returned to stripping, telling her husband that she missed the attention, the ego stroking, and the money.

Indeed, dancing in the Combat Zone was addictive for many women. By day, Heidi was a happy-go-lucky student at Simmons College in Boston. By night she was a punk rocker who hung out at the Rathskeller, a legendary music venue in Kenmore Square. Heidi had a friend who danced at the Naked i, and she would go with her to the strip club to hang out. With her thick black hair and smoky eyes, Heidi turned heads; the Naked i owner kept pushing her to dance. One day she lined up five Rusty Nail cocktails on the bar, downed them, and took a turn on the stage. "Frenchette," as she called herself, danced to punk music; her boyfriend, whom she later married, got a job as a disc jockey at the club. For Heidi, the scene at the Naked i was part of the alternative lifestyle: decadent, exhilarating, and dangerous. She was known as the "champagne girl" for her ability to get men to buy her expensive bottles of bubbly.

Getting men to buy drinks—called "mixing" or "mingling"— was the part of the job that wasn't advertised. In the Combat Zone's heyday, dancers were not tipped, as they are today—no slipping dollar bills into G-strings or tossing money on the stage. Instead, they were expected to mingle with customers between sets and persuade patrons to buy them drinks, which were usually overpriced and sometimes watered down. Dancers sidled up to customers and asked them, "Would you like some company? Would you like to buy me a drink?" If the men obliged, the dancers would sit down and chat. This mixing was part and parcel of a dancer's shift. If the customer paid seven dollars to buy a dancer a drink, the bartender got a dollar, the dancer got a dollar, and the house got five. Mixing was so profitable that the Naked i's owners didn't bother charging a cover fee; their logic was that it was far more lucrative to draw in consenting adults willing to pay the high prices for booze.

Dancers were given a quota for mixing, and if they didn't reach the drink quota, they didn't get their tips. Cocktails ranged from six to eight dollars at a time when a beer was only two dollars or less. Dancers often asked to have their drinks surreptitiously watered down, lest they would not be able to make it through the evening. "That was the money-maker part of the job," said Kendra Wilde. "You hustled drinks. Dancing was just the attraction for customers so they would buy you drinks." At first, Julie Jordan recalled, "It was not easy going up to strangers and asking them to buy you a drink knowing full well that they were being ripped off for seven dollars. I didn't have the maturity or insight to know that these guys knew exactly what they were doing ... They knew the game, they knew if they wanted you to sit with them they were going to have to put out that kind of money."

Lewin said it wasn't hard to make her quota; she often did so in the first half hour, but it added a layer of pressure for the dancers. Mixing made it more difficult to romanticize and glamorize exotic dancing because the girls were vulnerable to customers, not all of whom were well behaved despite the bouncers standing warily by. Dancers could not touch customers, but the need to push booze invited a stroke here or there—and possibly more than just a stroke. None of this was legal, of course, and clubs relied on those stone-faced bouncers to flash the lights when the cops arrived to pay a visit, warning the dancers to back away from customers.

Customers shelling out money to sit with the girls included local businessmen on lunch breaks, construction workers, college boys, conventioneers from the Midwest, husbands from the suburbs, the curious, and the regulars. Celebrities would sometimes pop in. Dancers recall seeing a polite James "Whitey" Bulger in the Naked i. Hit man Joe "The Animal" Barboza was often seen, reportedly while collecting "protection" money. And a few customers were simply folks who just wanted a drink after working a late shift, like the city's reporters. John Sloan, who came to know the Combat Zone intimately through his work for the BRA, asserted to *Boston Magazine* "the average customer in the Two O'Clock lounge is an electrical engineer who lives in Newton, is married, has two kids, and doesn't cheat on his wife."

Dancers may have had qualms about mixing with customers, but it was accepted as part of the job. And the job brought in money. Big

money. Performers made up to two hundred dollars a night or five to six hundred dollars a week, a huge amount in those days. "I lived in a condo. I had all the clothes I wanted," Wilde said. "It was a killing for my age," Julie Jordan said. "I rented a beautiful house in Nahant. I had no money troubles; I was able to give friends in need five grand without worries about getting it back." Heidi lived in a gorgeous loft. "I had everything you could imagine, all the clothes I wanted. It didn't last because of course we spent it." The dancers formed a kind of community, both friends and rivals. Heidi remembers the friendships. "You weren't dancing for the guys. You were dancing for yourself and for the other girls. We were so into ourselves. It was like a power trip," she said.

The duality of exotic dancing, as sexual object and erotic goddess, caught the attention of Yale professor Jessica Berson, a dancer and dance teacher. In her dissertation that became the book, *The Naked Result: How Exotic Dance Became Big Business*, she explores the conflicting messages of the striptease. "The story of the Combat Zone highlights both the pleasures of the 'authentic' and particular ways in which notions of authenticity can be constructed, torn down, and reassembled," she writes. "The borders of the Zone were artificial, imposed by a city government eager to contain the 'porno plague'—but the performances within the Zone erupted in creative freedom because of those very borders." It was a refuge for Onyx, for example. It was the mechanism by which some women got through school. Lewin funded her bachelor's and master's degrees by dancing, and later received a doctorate from Brown University. After a distinguished career at Suffolk University, she served as a dean at Arkansas State University, where she is now a history professor and the director of the Heritage Studies PhD program.

Despite her own experience as a dancer, Lewin, who interviewed exotic dancers for a graduate research project, considers strippers "sex workers," even if they didn't turn tricks. To her mind, they were selling themselves merely by using their body as a commodity. Her study found that many had been sexually abused as children. Drug and alcohol abuse was endemic. "The Combat Zone did not come out of the blue." It reflects the choices women made throughout history. Her memoir, *Naked is the Best Disguise*, was written in part to counteract the superficial and glamorized accounts of strippers in the media.

While some dancers were as calculating as any Wall Street stockbroker, some spiraled into drug addition, prostitution, and self-loathing. Indeed, "There were drugs. Yes, there was a lot of drugs," said Wilde. "Angel dust, coke. Customers would bring it in for the girls. I remember doing a lot of coke."

Lucy Wightman, a.k.a. Princess Cheyenne, saw dancing in the Combat Zone through a rosier lens. "I became a woman on the honey-colored stage of the Naked i," she wrote in 2010. "My memories are full with moving colors and group laughter. I never felt discomfort, anxiety, or fear."

Wightman went on to reinvent herself numerous times. She worked as radio talk-show host for "Ask Princess Cheyenne" on WBCN-FM and became a bodybuilder, winning amateur bodybuilding competitions. After finally leaving stripping, she worked as a counselor and therapist but encountered legal trouble for presenting herself as a psychologist without an official license, even though her clients insisted she was an insightful, thoughtful therapist. She was sentenced to a year of house arrest. Tragically, her only child, a daughter, was killed in a car accident in 2006. Wightman eventually became a professional photographer.

Kendra Wilde danced until she hurt her knee playing basketball and could not return to the stage. "What I liked was the money, the lifestyle. I loved the money. I liked the atmosphere. I was admired by everybody. I took all that for granted—not that I was a prima donna but I thought that was going to be the way it was. It was like being a rock star. Anything goes. 'Kendra Wilde. Kendra Wilde. I wish I was you.' But then it all ends. This is the hard part. The ending. You don't know how to end it." Heidi gave up stripping when she got pregnant but remained involved in the music business. She went on to work as a rock 'n' roll booking agent and later ran the Boston rock club Mavericks. After a host of different careers, she settled in upstate New York.

By the beginning of 1978, Julie Jordan was a far cry from the hippie chick who lived in a teepee. But she wasn't exactly Natalie Wood, either. Julie had money and notoriety, yet the cash was not soothing her inner conflicts. When the Blizzard of 1978 hit Boston in February of that year, Julie split for California, her stripping days over.

FACADE ELEVATION

Hoping to lighten the mood of the Zone, the BRA, under the direction of John Sloan, worked on drawing facades and schematics for businesses such as strip clubs and pornographic bookstores. Courtesy City of Boston.

CHAPTER 6

DEALING WITH THE DEVIL

1975 to 1976

....

This is probably the first time that an American city has rationally approached the question of 'adult entertainment' and has sought to ameliorate its impact, rather than remove it.

"BOSTON'S ADULT ENTERTAINMENT DISTRICT,"
BRA PAMPHLET, JANUARY 1976

T hat sign had to go. There was no doubt in the mind of architect John Sloan. Hired by the BRA in 1972, Sloan was given a plum assignment two years later: improve the appearance of the Combat Zone. Sloane was a graduate of the esteemed Pratt Institute in New York City. He was young, hip, brilliant, unconventional, brimming with ideas, and certain that he could tame the neon tastelessness snaking through Boston's downtown. By improving the lighting, signage, and storefronts and making the streets more seductive than scary, the Zone could be transformed to resemble a bawdy section of New Orleans. Or perhaps a miniature Las Vegas strip. That meant working with the clubs and their owners; luckily, Sloan found an ally in Debra Beckerman.

Sloan, Beckerman, Beckerman's assistant Lorie Beckelman, and others began holding regular planning meetings at the Two O'Clock Lounge. They talked about elevations and design specs while the strippers did their thing on stage. Beckerman was in agreement with Sloan: the two-story sign affixed to the side of the Liberty Tree Building right next to the Two O'Clock Lounge was an eyesore. The sign's owner, however, was not in agreement. In fact, he was downright uncooperative. So, Sloan came up with a plan.

In the pre-dawn gloom on a freezing January day in 1975, barely two months after the designation of the AED, Sloan and Beckerman met on Washington Street to commit an act of guerrilla urban renewal. Their target: the gigantic sign for the House of Pizza.

This was a caper befitting Sloan's eccentric style. When the city was offered a forty-foot-tall former ice cream stand in the shape of a huge milk bottle, he sought to place it at the relatively new City Hall Plaza. He was overruled. Fortunately, the dairy company Hood agreed to buy the giant milk bottle and restore it. It was eventually placed outside the Boston Children's Museum, where it remains today as a beloved icon. Sloan pushed for the creation of a pedestrian zone in Downtown Crossing, brushing off opposition by the police, fire, and public works departments. Later, he advocated for the placement of a gift from the government of Taiwan in Boston's Chinatown: a traditional Chinese ceremonial gate or "pailou." It was positioned just steps away from the half-razed Chinese Merchants Building. *Boston Magazine* called him a "visionary architect, [a] serious and totally committed master builder who has not lost his sense of whimsy." His brash style suited the tenor of Kevin White's administration.

At the time, Sloan believed in the process of urban renewal, a concept then being embraced by the country's city planners. The thought was that changing the physical areas of poor neighborhoods could combat poverty and social ills. "That's not exactly true," he now ruefully acknowledges, "but that was the theory at the time." The Zone's frontier of decaying storefronts, dilapidated buildings, and off-color businesses was an irresistible challenge for this urban pioneer.

Sloan envisioned a new look for the Zone's traditional businesses. He valued the balance between form and function. He came up with sparkling ideas for neon club signs that were more carnival and less carnal. He wanted to invoke a wink, a sense of amusement, and he encouraged the public to see the sex industry humorously. He tried to convince one bookstore owner to re-name an establishment "The

Dirty Bookstore," and he told the *Wall Street Journal*, "I'd love to do a sign called Sleazy Girls." Even the *Globe*'s renowned architecture critic, Robert Campbell, was impressed with the approach, noting that Sloan fought the good fight—and saw the potential in Boston's naughtiest neighborhood.

For someone who was holding regular design meetings at the Two O'Clock, Sloan's personal life was far from flashy. He drove a Volkswagen camper and was obsessed with his work. He didn't drink and he didn't do drugs. When he went to a party at Beckerman's house, he zeroed in on a plate of brownies; he loved brownies. Unknowingly, he ended up eating ten marijuana brownies and got so sick he had to be driven home.

To him, the biggest eyesore in the Zone was not the unapologetic façade of the Two O'Clock Lounge, nor the brazen Naked i logo. It was that egregiously large sign advertising the Greek-cuisine House of Pizza that operated from the first floor of the Liberty Tree Building. (Not to be confused with the Pasquale family's King of Pizza, in the Boylston Building across the street.) The sign was totally out of scale and loomed over the new Liberty Tree Park like a menacing cloud. But the owner of the House of Pizza, who rented the space, could not be convinced to take it down.

The intersection of Washington and Boylston Streets, the location of the House of Pizza eyesore. Courtesy City of Boston.

Sloan was not deterred. He wrote a letter to the Boston Building Department noting that the BRA had control of the area and that building permits should "come to us first," (which wasn't exactly true). He called the owner of the Liberty Tree Building and told him he wanted to take the sign down. "He says to me, 'It's not my sign.' I said, 'I understand, but it's your building. Would you agree that the sign should come down?' 'Well,' he says, 'Yeah, it's no skin off my nose. You can take the sign down. But you gotta deal with the pizza guy.' 'OK, as long as I have your permission to take the sign down.'"

He hired a sign removal company and asked them to show up in the middle of the night (supposedly out of concerns about traffic). Under Sloan's direction, the workers started taking down the sign. Halfway into the job, the pizza guy showed up, beside himself with rage. They argued. The owner called the police. The police showed up with lights and sirens blazing. Work was halted. The owner demanded Sloan be arrested. Sloan called police chief John Doyle. Doyle told him to call a lawyer. Sloan called a BRA lawyer. Then he called a friend at the Building Department to see if he could get the sign condemned. Eventually, the sign came down, leaving one outraged owner and one satisfied urban guerilla.

The next day, Sloan was called into BRA director Robert Kenney's office. He recalls the exchange: "'Why didn't you ask me before you did this?' And I said, 'because you would have said no. This way, you get to deny you knew anything about it.'" Better to beg forgiveness than ask permission. That was Sloan. He was not fired.

Sloan went on to design the new Liberty Tree Park, a triangular space carved out of Boylston Street where the corner with Washington was reconfigured. The spot became a monument to Boston's revolutionary history, featuring a striking copper replica of the famed Liberty Tree plaque (located on the third floor of the Liberty Tree Building across the street) set atop the red brick sidewalk. However, this new Liberty Tree Park was the only city park without benches, a deliberate decision made out of concern that the homeless would bed down there and hookers would take a load off.

Boston's porn "solution" began to draw nationwide attention. The BRA received inquiries from at least fifty cities, many of them struggling to deal with pornography proliferation. The *Wall Street*

Journal called the AED a "home on the raunch," a "sexual Disneyland," and a "stag sector." *Oui Magazine* heralded the Zone as "the new experiment in freedom that is Boston's gift to America's third century." Sloan's signage was praised as zippy, witty, and stylish. "The Combat Zone is actually starting to look like Fun City," *Boston Magazine* declared. "Hopefully in the end it will also look like Ghirardelli Square in San Francisco."

But while Teddy Venus, Beckerman's boss, saw the value in improving the image of the Zone, others balked. "None of the other club owners really agreed with that. They were too busy working" to attend meetings, Sloan said. More likely they were suspicious, knowing that this was an uneasy truce in the battle over the city's proclivities. So, despite efforts by Sloan and Beckerman, changes came only in bits and pieces.

On June 12, 1975, the new Liberty Tree Park was to be dedicated. At the last minute, Mayor Kevin White and other officials said they would not attend the ceremony. The BRA complained that the adult entertainment businesses were not living up to their part of the bargain in sprucing up their appearances. "What are they talking about," one Zone denizen told the *Boston Globe*. "We took down the big pizza sign, didn't we?" Instead, the indefatigable Debra Beckerman rounded up strippers from the Two O'Clock Lounge to be there. Barney Frank attended and gave a short speech, for which Sloan was always grateful.

Even as Sloan pressed on, contradictions emerged. The Zone was meant to contain legal adult entertainment, but plenty of illegal activities, including prostitution and drug dealing, were going on. (Barney Frank supported legalizing prostitution among consenting adults in the Zone, but his was a minority stance.) The cops were not surprised that hookers congregated near the clubs; that's where business was brisk. Moreover, it seemed that despite the declaration of AED supporters, pornography was not contained to lower Washington Street. The Pru Cinema on Boylston near the Prudential Building showed *Deep Throat* throughout the 1970s, and gay porn was screened at small theaters near South and North Stations. Still, Sloan, Beckerman, and others were convinced that the AED was working as planned.

In January 1976, the BRA published a slick, polished pamphlet on "Boston's Adult Entertainment District" that proudly "set out the

The intersection of Washington and Boylston Streets after the start of the BRA's improvement program and the construction of Liberty Tree Park. Note that the House of Pizza sign has been removed. Courtesy City of Boston.

rationale and the implementation process for a program designed to prevent the spread of adult entertainment activities and to upgrade the environment of the area where adult entertainment activities are now concentrated." Like a weight-loss brochure, the pamphlet confidently displayed before and after photos of Liberty Tree Park, one showing the huge House of Pizza sign in the background and the other without. The popular Essex Delicatessen was in the "before" photo; the "after" photo revealed it had been replaced by an adult entertainment site with an illuminated movie sign designed by Sloan. The pamphlet aimed to show how the porno beast could be reined in. There were clever architectural renderings for other possible businesses: The Show Bar, Macy Drug, and even The Dirty Bookstore. Page sixteen had a particularly fanciful design for an adult entertainment storefront that resembled a face, with the door leading through an open mouth. However, the mouth's lips formed an arch that more closely resembled female genitalia, as if Georgia O'Keeffe had been transplanted from the desert to Washington Street. The drawing reflected Sloan's theory that the Zone designs should have a sense of fun. Sloan's idea of fun did not fit that of his boss. After several thousand pamphlets were printed, BRA director Kenney saw this particular page and demanded the drawing be removed and the pamphlet reprinted.

Sloan kept his job, but this was probably the first time a Boston city-planning document was recalled for obscenity.

THE PATRIOTIC STRIPPER

I n the summer of 1976, with America's Bicentennial in full swing, all of Boston seemed to be decked out in red, white, and blue. Bostonians felt a keen ownership of the American Revolution—didn't it start under the Liberty Tree?—and even the Combat Zone was caught up in the celebration, preparing in its own carnal way for the visitors who would flock to the city. The pervasive patriotism gave costume designer Hedy Jo Star an idea for dancer Julie Jordan.

In those days, Combat Zone headline acts wore glittering, sequined gowns that cost thousands of dollars. Many stunners were made by Star; she was the go-to gal for fabulous outfits. Her signature style was well known among the dancers.

Star's personal history put her at ease in the Zone. She was born male into a large family in Oklahoma, and at the age of eighteen, she began the long process of transitioning to female. Her transition finally culminated in what she boasted was the first fully successful gender reassignment surgery in the United States in 1962.

Boston's top acts coveted Star's dresses. In early 1976, when Hedy Jo told Julie, "I think you should be Miss Bicentennial," Julie just laughed. "I thought that would be something—the patriotic stripper." But Hedy Jo had already sketched out the outfit, complete with top hat, cane, and bolero jacket. Being a non-traditionalist, Julie decided to buy the outfit. Miss Bicentennial turned out to be a hit.

Her act caught the attention of a pair of writers tasked with creating a special show for City Hall Plaza as part of the city's celebrations. Organizer Peter Bates, a poet and playwright, knew Julie Jordan through a mutual friend; he told his partner, Kevin Vandenbroek, "Kevin, let's

Julie Jordan performing in City Hall Plaza as Miss Bicentennial, 1976. Courtesy *Boston Herald*.

shake up this world a little bit." He and Kevin arranged for poetry and play readings, and also for Julie to perform as Miss Bicentennial.

Right on the grave of old Scollay Square, Julie honored the nation's birthday by stripping down to pasties and G-string to the music of John Philip Sousa. The crowd was stunned and enthralled. A *Boston Herald* photographer snapped a picture with a caption that read: "Julie Jordan does her thing in City Hall Plaza as part of a Bicentennial spoof. The spoof included [a] poetry reading but Julie attracted a lot more attention." Years later, after her father had died, Julie was surprised to find this newspaper clipping folded and tucked into her father's wallet.

Prostitutes outside Jacob Wirth on Stuart Street.
©Spencer Grant.

CHAPTER 7

THE SEDUCTION OF MAYOR WHITE

1975 to 1976

....

About three months after the adult entertainment district was established, Mayor Kevin White wanted a firsthand look. So, in February 1975, the city's highest official took a tour of the Combat Zone, supposedly incognito, but accompanied by his staff and *Boston Globe* reporter John B. Wood to ensure media coverage. The group hit the Two O'Clock Lounge, the Picc-a-dilly Lounge, the Mousetrap, the Teddy Bear Lounge, and The Other Side, a gay discothèque in Bay Village. A Two O'Clock bouncer stopped White's baby-faced press secretary, George Regan, assuming he was too young to enter, but otherwise the group got the full Combat Zone experience, including being hustled for drinks. "I spent eighty-one dollars in there," White complained at one point. On LaGrange Street, a young woman in yellow knickers and a feathered hat approached the mayor.

"You want some company?" she cooed.

"Thank you," said White. "I'm too old."

"Let me make you feel young," said the woman. But the mayor managed to escape unscathed.

"You know," White told Wood, "My idea of a city has room for these places. I don't condone everything that goes on here, but if they don't disturb the theaters or residential areas, what harm are they doing?"

What harm indeed?

◆

It worked like this: Walking through the Combat Zone, men would be swarmed by women close enough to smell their perfume or sweat. In the darkness of LaGrange Street, it was hard to tell how attractive the women were, but their cleavage was obvious and their legs went on forever. *Do you want company? Do you want a date?* One would come close, too close. Her hands were soft, insisting, touching a shoulder, an arm, and other, more intimate places. Even if the man hurried away, gently or not so gently shaking off the hands, refusing the entreaties, it was already too late. His wallet was gone. Who took it? The brunette with the short skirt and big, black-rimmed eyes? The coffee-and-cream colored girl with the plump crimson lips and hair that smelled of jasmine? Going back was useless because the girls would scatter, and pimps might be watching from the shadows. Approaching a cop would elicit a shrug. The smart fellows went home, either to tell or concoct a story. Unfortunately, not everyone was smart.

The fondle—perhaps even more than actual prostitution—came to define the Combat Zone in the late 1970s. Many of the street women "had such dexterity they could fondle a man and simultaneously remove his wallet," according to the *New York Times*. It was dangerous for men to resist. Police once recorded a man pushing aside a girl only to have her promptly put out a cigarette in his face, sending sparks flying into the night. Police and the press gave the girls a special name: "whorelets." Cops also called them "wolf packs."

These wolf packs were so good at pickpocketing that clubs in the area complained. Any client whose wallet was stolen on the way to the club would not be able to spend money on overpriced drinks. Even prostitutes complained, insisting female muggers gave legitimate hookers a bad name. Debra Beckerman, who was at this point much beleaguered, said that some women on the street had become "robber baron females" and insisted the situation was the fault of the police.

Beckerman's assertion would have made Boston police detective Billy Dwyer laugh had he heard it. A member of the city's vice control squad, he came to know the Combat Zone as well as any Boston law enforcement official could. He knew the cycle: girls arrested for prostitution were bailed out and back on the street, often in less than a day. He also knew of "mugger boys," guys who would follow a hooker and her trick and rob both.

In November of 1974, Dwyer came up with a scheme to deal with the problem of the wolf packs. A night scope camera was placed on an upper floor of the Union Warren Savings Bank on LaGrange Street. A half-dozen police decoys, including Dwyer, were deployed. From ten o'clock at night until a quarter past two in the morning, the decoys walked about, allowing their pockets to be picked as the camera recorded the action. Dwyer was robbed about six times and, knowing where the camera was filming, positioned himself where it was most advantageous for recording. He couldn't help looking up at the camera and smiling. "Even though I KNEW they were going to take the money out of my pocket, I never felt it," he said. The police didn't carry guns; they were supposed to be inebriated, and there was the danger a girl might reach in and grab a decoy's weapon. They also used their own money—that is, until Dwyer cut some paper into the shape of currency and shoved it in his pockets. One of his marks threw it back in his face.

On the night of the sting, the bars were letting out at a quarter past two. The police blocked off the area with their vehicles and moved in. The girls scattered, but the police were able to nab about fifty of them and herd them into a bus for processing.

For months afterward, Dwyer recalls with satisfaction, LaGrange was "like a graveyard. Safest place in town." A number of those arrested were never seen around the Zone again. To this day, Dwyer insisted that the busts more or less cleaned up the Zone. "We didn't have the hordes of girls and muggers on the street. It was relatively quiet."

Two years later, that quiet was shattered by a fatal incident that marked the beginning of the end for the Combat Zone.

Andrew Puopolo. Courtesy the Puopolo family.

CHAPTER 8

NOT SUPPOSED TO HAPPEN

1976

....

It was an event that pierced the protective bubble that everyone thought existed around all of us whether on campus or in Cambridge or Boston. It wasn't something that was meant to happen to Harvard undergraduates.

RICHARD WEISMAN, *HARVARD CRIMSON*

By 1976—almost exactly two years into the experiment of the adult entertainment district—the enthusiasm for Boston's Combat Zone was waning, even among its proponents. The district had been created for *legal* adult entertainment. Now many, particularly police officers, believed the Zone had turned into a true red-light district, a haven for prostitution, drug dealing, and other crimes. "The creation of the Zone has, by an irresistible logic, created a law enforcement nightmare," griped Suffolk County Assistant District Attorney Timothy O'Neil.

Detective Billy Dwyer's earlier crackdown hadn't exactly cleaned up lower Washington Street, but the area was quieter. Finger pointing continued among city agencies, the police, and the BRA about who was to blame for problems with this grand social experiment. Police groused that officers who maintained order at the clubs had been pulled out. BRA and city officials complained about a lack of law enforcement in the Zone and even hinted at corruption among the ranks of blue. And the rest of the city was still arguing about forced busing. In April, Stanley Foreman of the *Boston Herald American* had snapped a photo of an anti-busing protester appearing to stab a black man, attorney Ted Landsmark, with an American flag. Boston was being called the most racist city in America.

In October, Police Commissioner Robert diGrazia announced he was leaving for a better paying law enforcement position in Maryland. Although diGrazia had brought changes to Boston's entrenched police department, he had also thoroughly antagonized the rank-and-file. So much so that a representative of the police union derided him as getting all of his reform ideas from the cop show *Adam 12*. He had also lost the support of Mayor White. His four-year legacy would ultimately be regarded as a mix of success and failure.

But diGrazia had one last card to play. Just days before he left in early November, he released a 572-page report detailing corruption in the Boston Police Department, a final farewell—or finger—to the city. The report outlined patterns of "corruption and/or incompetence" among the police of District One, where the Combat Zone was located. This included taking payoffs from businesses and associating with prostitutes. Police officers were infuriated by the public release of the report; many blamed diGrazia for failed leadership, citing his alleged mixed signals about enforcement in the AED. Superintendent-in-Chief Joseph Jordan was tapped to replace diGrazia, and among his priorities was cleaning up the Zone. He took over on Monday, November 15, 1976, the day the Combat Zone took a critical step toward its ignominious end.

◆

Harvard University's 1976 football season was supposed to be glorious. It turned out to be a disappointment. Favored to win the Ivy League title, Harvard instead finished 4-3 in the league and 6-3 overall, with a final 21-7 drubbing by Yale on November 13th. A photo of cornerback Andrew Puopolo, head in hands, appeared in the *Boston Globe* over the headline: "The nightmare was Harvard's—it never awoke."

The middle of three children born to Andrew and Helen Puopolo,

Andrew Puopolo was both streetwise and book smart. Andy tested into the Boston Latin School, where he played three sports, including football. The five-foot-ten, 165-pound player was accepted into Harvard with an athletic scholarship.

Football was just one part of Andy's life at Harvard. He wanted to be a doctor so he majored in biology, and by November of his senior year, the twenty-one-year-old had already been accepted into two medical schools. The sad finish to the football season was only a minor disappointment on his way to graduation. Even so, he was among the fifty football players celebrating the end of the season with a traditional "breaking training" dinner at the Harvard Club in Boston on Monday, November 15, 1976. It was a fine affair that finished around eleven o'clock in the evening. And that's when many of the players embarked on another tradition: a trip to the Naked i.

The players broke into groups for the short drive from Back Bay to lower Washington Street, and after parking, hustled inside the club. Teammate Stewart K. Shofner would later describe the night to the *Harvard Crimson*, the college newspaper, as a raucous, no-holds-barred evening. "By the end of the night, the Harvard football team had taken over the stage—stripping off their clothes, dancing with the girls. In our mindset, we were taking over that part of the city. Testosterone-driven, fueled by alcohol—we were confident." At two o'clock in the morning, the club closed and the Harvard players spilled out onto Washington Street.

Elsewhere in the Combat Zone, forty-one-year-old Leon J. Easterling, thirty-six-year-old Richard S. Allen, Easterling's half-brother, and thirty-three-year-old Edward Joseph Soares were hanging out. Each had a lengthy criminal record: Allen had been arrested at least fifty times, Easterling more than forty times, and Soares about a dozen times. Charges included larceny, unarmed robbery, and drug-related crimes. According to some law enforcement sources, Easterling was known as a pimp, but his actual role has never been made clear. Allen worked as a kind of bouncer at the Carnival Lounge, a bar on Boylston Street. Soares sold jewelry on the sidewalk. The Zone, in all its seedy glory, was their territory, their neighborhood. They felt as comfortable on lower Washington Street as the Harvard players did in Harvard Yard.

There were also two women in the Combat Zone that night who were, according to law enforcement sources, hoping to score money for drugs. They were sixteen-year-old Cassandra McIntyre and twenty-two-year-old Naomi J. Axel, both black. When a group of drunken white guys in suits and ties stumbled out of the Naked i, they sensed an easy target.

What happened next has been the subject of a variety of accounts, interpretations, and conflicting witness statements made under oath. Nearly all the Harvard players were white, Easterling and Allen were black, and Soares was Latino, so the event and the aftermath took on racial overtones in a city already rife with racial tension. The bare outline of events has been well established, but the nuances are more difficult to determine. What's clear is that everything happened quickly, and within twenty minutes, lives were ruined forever.

After leaving the Naked i, Andrew Puopolo stopped at Tony Pasquale's King of Pizza for a slice. Meanwhile, team manager Chester Stone and a group of players headed for his van. This group was solicited by a number of women, including Axel and McIntyre, who followed the players to the van. One of the girls jumped in (or was invited inside). When the girls finally left, defensive tackle Charles Kaye realized his wallet was missing.

It should have ended there. But Kaye wanted his wallet back. So, he and two other players jumped out of the van to chase the two women, who ran along Boylston Street toward Washington Street. The players did not get far. Emerging from an alley called Bumstead Court near the Carnival Lounge, a man appeared and blocked their way. The man, later identified as Allen, yelled at the players. Kaye and the two others sized up the situation and returned to the van, deciding it was too dangerous.

It could have ended there. But one of the players in the van spotted Axel and shouted, "There she goes!" The van turned into an alleyway next to the Silver Slipper at 22 Boylston and some of the players jumped out to once again chase Axel.

About this time, Puopolo, Stephen Saxon, and other teammates were making their way up Boylston Street; only then did they become aware that some kind of incident was going on. They confronted Axel, who turned around and ran screaming up Boylston Street toward Tremont Street, pursued by both groups of players.

A number of players caught up to Axel at the intersection of Tremont and Boylston Streets. According to court records, she fell to the ground as the pursuers caught up to her. Saxon pulled her to her feet but she took off again, running south on Tremont toward LaGrange Street. The night had taken an ugly turn.

From somewhere in the vicinity, Soares emerged. (He, Allen, and Easterling later claimed they got involved to help Axel.) Soares knocked Saxon down. As Saxon got to his feet, other players moved to confront Soares, who kicked at the advancing players but backed off across Tremont toward Boston Common. Allen now reappeared, yelling furiously, "Get out of here. You came to the Zone and got burned." From the other side of Tremont, Soares took off his jacket and cried, "Come on, I've been waiting for this."

Just as player Thomas Lincoln, realizing the situation was out of control, yelled, "Let's get out of here," Easterling entered the scene from Boylston, brandishing a knife. Another player saw the gleam of the steel in Easterling's hand and screamed a warning. Seconds later Easterling was beside Lincoln and, according to court testimony, he stabbed Lincoln in the arm and abdomen. Lincoln fell backwards, clutching his stomach. Other players helped Lincoln back to the van while Puopolo, Saxon, and a third player went back to Saxon's car on Boylston.

Later, Lincoln would testify he saw Easterling, Soares, Allen, and a white or Hispanic man in a red jacket following the retreating players. Lincoln and a teammate also testified that the men shouted threats and taunts, "We're going to cut you white motherfuckers." The four men passed Saxon's car and moved toward the van, where about fifteen players were present. The man in the red jacket opened the van door and pulled Charlie Kaye out by his tie and Soares punched him.

Puopolo, seeing Kaye attacked, jumped into the fray. At one point, Soares and Puopolo traded blows. As Soares wrestled with Puopolo, Easterling struck over Soares' shoulder with a knife, slicing Soares' knuckle and hitting Puopolo's arm and chest. Puopolo and Soares tumbled onto the sidewalk. The men got up and player Scott Coolidge managed to separate them. Andy muttered, "I'm all right. Let's get out of here." But Coolidge saw his teammate's shirt was soaked with blood. Coolidge testified that Easterling then shouted at Puopolo and when Puopolo turned toward him, Easterling stabbed him one more time in the chest. Easterling, Soares, Allen, and the man in the red jacket fled; Easterling discarded the knife.

At about this moment, two police officers saw Puopolo and Coolidge staggering down the street. Puopolo collapsed in Coolidge's arms, blood running from his mouth. Puopolo was rushed to the Tufts-New England Medical Center, which was just blocks away, arriving by 2:23 a.m.

At the hospital, Andy Puopolo had no pulse; his heart's right ventricle was pierced. Working quickly, surgeons were able to make some repairs but the damage was immense. Puopolo went into a coma and was placed on a respirator. Lincoln was treated for his stab wounds at Massachusetts General Hospital and was discharged a few days later. Police apprehended Easterling, Soares, and Allen, who were identified by other Harvard players; Soares was taken to a hospital to have his knuckles treated. The man in the red jacket was never found or arrested. And a day later, Kaye's wallet was found in the vicinity, empty of the ten dollars it had held.

For the next month, Puopolo remained in a coma as his devastated parents and siblings stayed by his side. The city held its breath, too. "Make me a miracle, God," pleaded Helen Puopolo as she kissed her son's lifeless hand. Andrew's younger brother Danny sat by his bedside and talked to him, hoping for a flutter of the eyelids, any kind of movement.

The attack drew national attention. Civic fury now focused on the Zone. In an editorial, the *Boston Globe*, which had supported the concept of the adult entertainment district, called on Mayor White to clean up the area. South Boston representative Raymond Flynn furiously called the area Boston's "terminal cancer zone." Flynn railed: "The people of Boston are outraged at what has been allowed to exist by the city administration under the guise of constitutional rights. Whose rights are we protecting? The underworld? Organized crime? Pimps? Pornographers? Dope pushers?" Jan Brogan, then a journalism student at Boston University, recalled the city's mood. "I remember the tension in the city," she said. "An anger that you could feel coming up from the street like heat."

Debra Beckerman attempted damage control and blamed police for not patrolling in the late hours. "The area is being used by the police as a whipping boy. Yes, there are problems here but the problems are out on the streets and not in the club," she told an unconvinced Jeremiah Murphy of the *Boston Globe*.

A month later, on December 17th, just after four o'clock in the morning, Puopolo suffered cardiac arrest and died. With tears streaming down his face, Andrew Puopolo Sr. told reporters his son was like a flower that was cut down. Thousands gathered for his funeral a few days later; members of the football team were honorary pallbearers.

Easterling, Soares, and Allen faced murder charges. They maintained they acted under threat. Allen said he was trying to help a black woman being chased by a group of white men, and Easterling said he jumped in to protect his half-brother, Allen. Their defense lawyers argued that a brawl among a group of men simply got out of hand.

District Attorney Thomas Mundy took an aggressive approach for prosecution. Because of the way the night unfolded in a series of confrontations, Easterling, Allen, and Soares were charged with "engaging in a joint or common enterprise" in the premeditated killing of Puopolo. That meant all three men were charged with first-degree murder, including Allen, who had not had verbal or physical contact with Puopolo.

Barely three months after Puopolo's death, the trial began in Suffolk Superior Court with jury selection. Both the defense and prosecution attempted to get a jury sympathetic to their side. Using peremptory challenges, the prosecutors eliminated twelve of thirteen black jurors while the defense cut seventeen potential jurors with Italian last names. The final jury had one black juror and no Italians. Prosecutors described the three defendants as "protectors" of a group of "robber whores" who acted out when one of the girls lifted a wallet. The lawyers for the accused argued that the death resulted from a brawl instigated by the Harvard students.

In painful, tearful testimony, Puopolo's teammates described the events of that night and how a sobbing Coolidge cradled his injured teammate's head in his lap. On the stand, Axel denied taking Kaye's wallet but acknowledged that she and a friend followed the players to the van. Soares testified that he was "riled up" when he fought with Puopolo but that none of his punches landed: "I let go. I swear to God he was still standing." Easterling acknowledged in his testimony that he stabbed Puopolo and Lincoln but said he was only trying to defend Soares and panicked. "I didn't want to see Eddie get hurt. I jumped up in the air to hit Mr. Puopolo with my knife and yelled to let him alone," he said. He broke down saying, "I'm sorry about Mr. Puopolo. At the time, I didn't realize how serious it was. I'm awfully sorry this happened."

Meanwhile, Andrew's younger brother, Danny, seethed. People were asking why Andrew was in the Combat Zone in the first place. "I burn up," he told a reporter. "It was a kind of tradition for most of the Harvard team to go down for the fun of it after the windup dinner. They weren't looking for trouble. And Andy was just trying to help another fellow."

On March 24, 1977, after brief deliberation, a jury found Easterling, Soares, and Allen guilty of first-degree murder. Judge James C. Roy of Suffolk Superior Court sentenced the trio to life in prison with no chance of parole. Allen's attorney, Henry F. Owens, complained to a reporter, "If it had been a black student from Roxbury Community College [who was killed], the affair would have been handled differently." The Puopolo family felt scant relief at the verdict. Their grief over Andy's sudden and horrible death could not be wholly assuaged by the legal system.

Lawyers for the convicted trio appealed, focusing on the composition of the jury. Although the foreman of the jury was black, the lawyers argued that during the jury empanelment the prosecutor struck "ninety-two percent of the available black jurors, and only thirty-four percent of the available white jurors." This deprived the defendants of their right to a fair trial and an impartial jury, they claimed. The state's highest court agreed, and a new trial was ordered.

Late in 1979, the case was retried. In the years since the original verdict, Boston remained dogged by its reputation for racial hatred. A week before jury selection was scheduled to begin, Darryl Williams, a fifteen-year-old black football player from Jamaica Plain, was shot and nearly killed during a game at Charlestown High School. Williams had just completed his first varsity pass. Three white boys on a nearby roof were accused of the shooting. They said they had been shooting at pigeons, but many believed it was racially motivated; Charlestown was a tight-knit, mostly white section of Boston and residents there had seethed with resentment against court-ordered busing. Williams survived but was permanently paralyzed.

Such events are not supposed to affect juries. But in a stunning reversal in the second trial, Easterling was convicted of manslaughter and Soares and Allen were acquitted and released. Easterling was sentenced to eighteen to twenty years in prison. He served his time and was eventually paroled.

"The verdicts see-sawed in the extreme, and the Puopolo family was left feeling that their son did not receive justice. One of the many tragedies of this story is that Andy's name became associated with Boston's racist history, while he was the victim in all of it, and from all accounts he had the best racial relations on his team," said Brogan, the journalism student turned author. (Brogan is at work on a book, *Murder in the Combat Zone,* about the case.) The "technicality" that overturned the first verdict became a precedent-setting decision that changed the way Boston picked its juries, she said.

Easterling, Soares, and Allen have since died. Darryl Williams became a motivational speaker and an advocate for ending racial hatred and violence. He died at the age of forty-six. As the years go by, the details of just how a Harvard student came to be murdered in the Zone have become fuzzy. Few remember that Puopolo was not an instigator of the events, only someone who jumped in to help a fellow teammate.

Both Andrew's brother and sister had sons they named Andrew. Every year, Harvard football alumni play a game of touch football against Yale and donate the money raised to a scholarship named for Andrew Puopolo. A park on Commercial Street in the North End has been dedicated to Andrew Puopolo's memory. The family continues to grieve. "I don't think any of us has been the same since. Every one of us has been emotionally broken," said Andrew's sister, Francesca.

Prostitutes stopping traffic.
Courtesy *Boston Herald*.

CHAPTER 9

DANGER ZONE

1977 to 1984

....

Glitter may be one part of the image of the Zone, but danger is as much a part of that image. For many people danger, rather than being an inhibiting factor, is part of the attraction of the Zone—it makes it more exciting and adventurous...

BRA THEATER AND ENTERTAINMENT DISTRICT REPORT, 1979

T he Puopolo case was heart wrenching, but it was not the only sensational murder associated with the Combat Zone. Two other murders, each happening miles away from the area, were tied to the Zone's sex-for-hire business. Both cases deeply affected Vice Squad Detective Billy Dwyer.

Dwyer remembers when he met Robin Nadine Benedict in 1982. He and his partner were on top of almost everything going on in the Zone. "All the players knew who we were and when we appeared it was like the parting of the Red Sea," he recalled. "I expected to be shown the appropriate respect. I was the *man* and I wasn't going to be treated like I was stupid by some new face who didn't understand the street protocol." Those were the rules of the game.

Benedict ignored those rules. When Dwyer noticed an attractive young woman with dark hair and large brown eyes repeatedly going in and out of Good Time Charlie's on LaGrange Street, the epicenter of prostitution in the Combat Zone, Dwyer decided to stop and question her. He had no doubt she knew who he was, at least by reputation.

Benedict was cool but "a little snotty," acting annoyed at Dwyer's questions. She told him she was a writer doing research, not a hooker, and waved off his suggestions that she stay clear of the area. Her curt attitude didn't sit well with him. Benedict thought she had all the answers.

Benedict grew up in Methuen, one of five children of hardworking parents. She displayed a talent for art at an early age and attended the Rhode Island School of Design. By the early 1980s, she had, in the words of the authorities, "become attracted to a lifestyle that included prostitution."

Miles away in the prosperous suburb of Sharon lived William H.J. Douglas, a forty-something distinguished professor of anatomy at Tufts University School of Medicine. With a wife and three children and a prestigious job, Douglas seemed a model citizen. But he had a secret life that included trysts with a Combat Zone prostitute named Nadine.

According to a variety of sources, Douglas met Nadine Benedict in the Combat Zone and became infatuated, paying her hundreds of dollars and writing her loving and anguished letters. Benedict, however, was not ready to jettison what was likely a lucrative career as a hooker. Douglas began to steal money from Tufts to pay for his passion—nearly $70,000, according to some accounts.

The affair was both tragic and pathetic. At first Douglas and Benedict seemed to have an arrangement like any man and mistress, with payments, arguments, breakups, and reconciliations, most at the usual rate of fifty dollars per hour. Benedict, who was involved with a man who may have acted as her pimp, pulled away. Douglas stalked her, and he even tipped the police off to her activities with other clients. On March 5, 1983, the twenty-one-year-old Benedict vanished. Her anguished father—in denial about his beloved daughter's profession—sought out a reporter from the *Boston Herald*, asking for helping in publicizing the disappearance. An investigation showed that on that day, Benedict made a trip to Douglas's Sharon home, and he told investigators she dropped off drawings that she had done for his research work.

Soon after, a bloodstained hammer, a jacket identified as belonging to Benedict, and a shirt apparently belonging to Douglas were found at a rest area along Interstate 95. On March 19, the Douglas home was searched and items related to Benedict were found. Her body, however, remained missing. Even so, in November 1983, Douglas was charged with first-degree murder in Benedict's death. Prosecutors alleged that Douglas crushed Benedict's skull and disposed of the body in a dumpster headed for a landfill. In 1984, Douglas pleaded guilty to manslaughter, confessing to killing Benedict in a rage and stashing her body in a dumpster in Rhode Island. Not surprisingly, the tale of the prostitute and the professor made national headlines and produced at least two books. But the pain caused to each of the families was immeasurable.

Dwyer wonders how Douglas, a seemingly intelligent man, could have made the obvious mistakes that led to his arrest. Why did he include his own plaid shirt in the same bag as Benedict's beige corduroy jacket? And why did he leave incriminating evidence in his home, including Benedict's address book, driver's license, and red panties?

Douglas was paroled on June 3, 1993, after serving nearly ten years of an eighteen- to twenty-year sentence. That year, the *Boston Globe* reported that Douglas agreed to pay $20,000 to the parents of Robin Benedict, and to share with them half of any revenue he might receive from retelling the tale of the killing. Robin Benedict's body has never been found.

◆

From high-class courtesans to streetwalkers, the life of a Combat Zone hooker was a dangerous career. Prostitution was centered on LaGrange, but it extended through the Zone and Chinatown. Women in boots and short skirts stopped traffic to proposition drivers or waylaid pedestrians, even elderly couples. "You had hookers lining both sides of the street; there would be a constant line of traffic circulating the block. It was a show to see, it really was," recalled Dwyer. Many of the prostitutes—including some boys—were underage or runaways. Many were drug addicts. Some were addicted to the money.

From 1974 to 1977, at least four prostitutes associated with the Zone were murdered, their cases never solved. In June of 1977, a seventeen-year-old Sudbury girl, who had been working as a prostitute in the 663 Lounge, a Combat Zone bar, was found strangled in a Back Bay apartment. Judy Belfrey was a high school junior, in Boston for an "alternative semester," and was living with another woman at a Back Bay apartment. According to witnesses, a man in a maroon jacket offered Belfrey fifty dollars to go with him to the apartment. When she didn't return to the bar, police were notified. Her body was found in the apartment, but the case was never solved.

Zakia Lamrini was another Combat Zone prostitute who got in over her head.

Billy Dwyer knew all about the petite, dark-haired woman who called herself Rita Owens, among other aliases. She gave her age variously as nineteen, twenty, and twenty-one. She had come to the United States from Morocco to live with an uncle in Ohio and had gotten mixed up with a pimp who convinced her that selling her body was a path to the American dream. "I had arrested her a number of times," Dwyer recalled. "The last time I arrested her, the judge told her that if she were arrested again she was going to go to prison in Framingham for six months and she was going to do every day of it. So, she got the message. She told her pimp she couldn't work anymore and he beat the shit out of her." That's when she turned to Dwyer for help. He agreed to arrest the pimp if she stuck with the case rather than disappearing when it was time to testify (as so many did). She obliged, and the pimp got jail time. Rita, meanwhile, found a job dancing at the Mousetrap while living in Revere, Massachusetts, a working-class city north of Boston. She wasn't hooking anymore. Dwyer really believed that. But in March of 1981, she made a foolish decision when a man, whom Dwyer described as a former trick, met her in a Tremont Street coffee shop and offered her a ride to Revere. Dwyer later received a hysterical call from Rita, who told him that the man had driven her to somewhere outside the city and tried to rape her. She fought him off with a knife and then drove his car some distance away to a public phone, called a taxi, and abandoned the car. She wasn't sure what happened to the man, nor even where she had been attacked. What should she do?

Dwyer made a few calls, but no one knew of any man being stabbed. Then the body of George Karkiozis, a thirty-four-year-old fisherman from Somerville and father of three, was found in a parking lot at the Sandy Beach recreation area on Mystic Lakes in Winchester. He had been stabbed to death. Dwyer only learned about the body when he got a call from the Metropolitan District Commission Police Department looking for Rita. Dwyer told Rita to come to the Boston Police Headquarters, which she did. "She had finger marks around her neck like a guy tried to strangle her. She was disheveled. She didn't know what happened. She didn't realize the guy was that hurt."

Owens was arrested and tried for murder in 1982. She insisted that Karkiozis had tried to rape her and when she resisted, he began to strangle her. She always carried a small knife and testified that she stabbed him when he kept "coming at [her]." The medical examiner testified that Karkiozis had thirty-two stab wounds, twenty-eight of them in his back. Dwyer testified on Owens' behalf against the Commonwealth, an uncomfortable position that did not endear him to the prosecution.

A jury convicted Owens of first-degree murder, perhaps responding to the prosecution's contention that the twenty-eight stab wounds in the back constituted "extreme atrocity." She was sentenced to life in prison. In July of 1984, the Massachusetts Supreme Judicial Court overturned the murder conviction and life sentence due to a prosecution error and ordered a new trial. She was convicted of manslaughter, served time in prison, was paroled in the late 1980s, and moved away from Boston.

Three years after Dwyer retired in 2000 and moved to Las Vegas, Rita called him. Now a mother, she was living in Ohio. "I just wanted to thank you," she said. "I know the price you paid for testifying for me." The pair chatted for about ten minutes or so and that was that. It seemed to Dwyer that she had been able to turn her life around.

NO ONE
UNDER
21
ALLOWED

CHAPTER 10

THE CONSTITUTION AND THE COMBAT ZONE

....

The Constitution depends on defending even the most offensive people. If we encourage a litmus test for someone to have access to the courts, we endanger the whole legal system.

REGINA QUINLAN, *BOSTON GLOBE*, **MAY 3, 1992**

E arly in her life, Regina Quinlan felt the pull of a higher power. Born in Brookline and raised in Brighton, Quinlan was called to the religious life after graduating high school in 1960. Joining the Sisters of St. Joseph, Quinlan found herself surrounded by strong, dedicated women concerned about poverty and social ills. After graduating from Regis College in 1965, she spent four years teaching at Catholic schools but eventually began to believe that her path lay outside religious life. "Things were changing. It was time and I knew it," she recalled decades later.

In 1969, she left the Sisters of St. Joseph. Her father was an attorney who ran his own legal publishing company and two of her brothers were also attorneys. Quinlan decided she, too, would go to law school. She spent her days working and doing research for other lawyers and her nights attending Suffolk Law School. She graduated in 1973 and passed the Massachusetts bar that summer. One of her early achievements included helping another lawyer develop a defense strategy for a Combat Zone bookstore charged with distributing obscene magazines. If the magazines were defined as "books," she reasoned, this would make a stronger First Amendment case. The case, *Commonwealth v. Zone Books*, went all the way to the Massachusetts Supreme Judicial Court, which sided with the defense.

In 1978, in a leap of faith, she and two other attorneys opened a law office on Beacon Street in Boston, believing that somehow they would attract the cases and the clients to support their new quarters. It was a bold decision. The young lawyers threw an open house and invited everyone they knew to celebrate the move. The first to arrive was John Pino, a well-connected and prosperous attorney. Unknown to all, he had recently been appointed as a municipal court judge and would have to give up representing individual clients.

The next day, Pino called Quinlan, impressed by her quiet strength and emerging legal acumen. Pino explained his impending appointment to her. "Would you like some clients?" he asked. "Now, think about if you can represent them. If you have a problem with this, don't take them."

Quinlan jumped at the opportunity. She received seven hundred pending cases and seven hundred items of pornographic material—books, films, and magazines—seized by authorities from four or five Combat Zone bookstores. At that time, charges could be brought against the store clerk and the storeowner for possession of obscene material and/or possession with intent to disseminate obscene material. This meant that if police confiscated three hundred items, as many as six to nine hundred charges could be brought forth. So Quinlan's first step was to advance the idea of "simultaneous possession" to reduce the number of offenses. The seven hundred cases were reduced to seven complaints. She eventually took the case to trial and won, giving the young lawyer experience arguing before a jury.

That was just the start. Although Quinlan handled a variety of legal matters, she became well known as a staunch defender of the First Amendment as it applied to the lurid magazines, books, films, and paraphernalia sold in bookstores. Her clients did not include the Combat Zone's strip clubs or movie theaters, but she was kept busy. "At the time there were a lot of raids," she recalled.

Though lower Washington Street was zoned for adult entertainment, there was an ever-shifting line between what was permitted and what was obscene under the guidelines set by the Supreme Court in *Miller v. California*. City officials were also employing other weapons against Zone businesses such as entertainment and liquor licensing requirements and building codes.

After the Andrew Puopolo murder in 1976, the BRA's zeal for cooperating with Zone businesses vanished. City officials and the BRA were now bent on shrinking the Zone; it could not be eliminated, but the city could make it as difficult as possible for the X-rated industry to operate.

Quinlan was not the only attorney representing Zone businesses. Kenneth H. Tatarian was another, though perhaps the best-known obscenity defense attorney was Morris Goldings, who specialized in sensational cases. He represented boxer Marvelous Marvin Hagler, New England Patriots tackle Brian Holloway, and Harry "Doc" Sagansky, a well-known bookie and organized crime figure. He also represented the Naked i and Bel-Art Realty, which oversaw several strip clubs.

Goldings reveled in the public attention that came with having distinguished—if sleazy—clients. The firm he co-founded in 1961, Mahoney, Hawkes & Goldings, fearlessly took on notable cases. In one instance, the firm defended fifteen clients charged after police raided nearly every porn movie house and bookstore in the Zone. He insisted that the practice of dancers mingling or mixing with club patrons was protected under the constitutional right of free association. Besides, he argued, the clubs could not make a profit without the practice. A city licensing commissioner described Goldings as the "little bulldog" because he never gave up.

In 1989, when Goldings represented the Naked i against twelve licensing violations, he railed against the development forces that would eventually put the club out of business, declaring to the *Boston Globe*, "If an era ends, it'll be neither with a bang nor a whimper."

In 2001, Goldings was accused of stealing $17 million entrusted to him by clients and colleagues. After an investigation by the FBI and the United States Attorney's office, his license to practice law was suspended and he faced a slew of charges. At his 2002 trial, the *Globe* reported that Goldings, "using the stentorian voice that won him hundreds of cases across the nation … called himself a 'financial terrorist' and threw himself at the mercy of the federal judge who accepted his plea of guilty." He was sentenced to three years in prison. Goldings' downfall still bewilders colleagues.

Regina Quinlan's legal style was more understated, though equally formidable when representing clients. She found the material in the stores she represented to be profoundly distasteful. Yet obscenity, she argued, is difficult to define. Show the same film to two juries and the results will differ. "This is pure trash, I would say that to a jury. But we are talking about the right to choose. I don't want to read it. You don't want to read it. But there are adults who do," she argued. "I wasn't an advocate for pornography. I was a lawyer. It wasn't my role to judge either the people who were doing it or the people who were using it." Some of her fellow Sisters of St. Joseph were shocked when they learned she defended dirty bookstores. Others just laughed. "They knew me," she said.

In 1981, she successfully argued that the City of Boston's refusal to renew peep show licenses for three Combat Zone bookstores was unconstitutional. That same year, she represented Liberty Books Inc., when the business was forced from the Boylston Building and relocated to the former home of the State Theater at 613-615 Washington Street. When the Boston Licensing Division tried to stop the move, arguing that only about ten feet of the new site was inside the designated Combat Zone area, she led the challenge, winning a decision with the argument that "in the Zone, ten feet is as good as a whole building."

In 1982, she fought off an effort to force the disclosure of the names of bookstore owners and stockholders on First Amendment grounds, saying the disclosure would have a "chilling" effect on the businesses. She considers this one of her most significant cases, and to this day she declines to identify the owners, although their names have been reported by other sources.

The new Liberty Book Shop became what Quinlan humorously called a "porno palace." with two adult-movie houses, 112 peep-show booths, and seven "rap booths," which allowed patrons to talk through a glass partition with a nearly nude woman who performed three minutes of "erotic poses" for a few bucks. Quinlan's last adult entertainment case came in 1992 when she represented a video store in Springfield, Massachusetts. Authorities seized 355 potentially obscene publications. Seeking inspiration for her final argument before the Superior Court jury, Quinlan cited a quote carved into the granite side of the District Courthouse where the trial was held. The quote began, "In America we believe in the right to choose." She read that to the jury and concluded, "Tell the prosecutor we don't ban books in Springfield." The jury agreed. The complaints were dismissed.

Later that year, Quinlan's name was put forth for the post of Associate Justice of the Superior Court. A citizens group, Morality in Media, immediately raised objections that Quinlan had represented purveyors of pornographic material and had a "blemished" reputation. It didn't matter: she was confirmed by a 6-0 vote. In 1994, the new judge returned to Regis College to give the commencement address.

After twenty distinguished years on the bench, Quinlan retired. Interviewed in her cluttered, cozy apartment, she discussed her Combat Zone years with calm, carefully considered words. Did her defense prolong the life of the Combat Zone? She doesn't hedge. "Sure," she said. Quinlan maintains that constitutionally, the city had no choice but to establish the adult entertainment district. Every now and then, her otherwise even voice would rise in defense of the First Amendment and her eyes would ignite as she recalled the odder moments of that era. To this day, every Christmas, one of the bookstore's bookkeepers sends her a fruit basket.

Regina Quinlan as young nun and as associate justice of the Superior Court. Left, courtesy Regina Quinlan. Right, courtesy *Boston Herald.*

CHAPTER 11

UNREPENTANT

1976 to 1980

....

The Combat Zone was supposed to go belly up and in a sense it has. The belly can be seen seven nights a week vibrating sensuously on a fur rug in the middle of a polished wood runway in the center of a crowd of generally thick-waisted, usually stupefied gentlemen patrons.

BOSTON GLOBE, **FEBRUARY 12, 1979**

M any Bostonians like to say that the Combat Zone died with Andrew Puopolo, the Harvard football player stabbed to death in November of 1976. The tragedy certainly sent a chill through city planners who had thought this X-rated beast could be safely contained in its neon cage. The businesses of the Combat Zone didn't get the memo, though. They carried on, unrepentant and unapologetic. Many people who worked in the area have said they were saddened by Andrew Puopolo's death, but they were not overly affected by it. The Combat Zone was a tough place for people with tough lives. And the show went on.

Yet something had changed. John Sloan, the BRA architect who had worked with the clubs to spruce up their exteriors, said that after the Puopolo murder, BRA staffers were pulled from their Combat Zone work at the direction of Kenney and Mayor White. "I knew it was all over when that happened," Sloan recalled. "The murder was tragic and should never have happened. Violence ended this experiment." In the months that followed, the BRA shifted from reluctant ally of Combat Zone businesses to hardened foe. No more Liberty Tree rebranding. No more meetings at the Two O'Clock Lounge. No more intricate elevations for dirty bookstores. Game over. Declared Timothy O'Neil, Suffolk County assistant district attorney: "We were always opposed to it. We said it wouldn't work and it didn't."

Boston couldn't quite figure out what to do. "The effort to move Boston closer to utopia, first by quarantining and then by shrinking the Combat Zone, was rife with contradiction," as researchers Schaefer and Johnson noted. At the end of December 1976, the Boston Licensing Board voted to allow nude dancing in the Zone. (It had been officially banned in 1973, not that anyone noticed.) Dancers were required to stay two feet away from patrons and "mingling" was prohibited. Some, like Dan O'Brian, a *Herald American* columnist, applauded the move saying, "It would remove from police the burden of having to arrest performers, allowing them to concentrate on more worrisome violations."

And those worrisome violations were many.

In October 1977, Police Commissioner Joseph Jordan approved a series of raids intended to find material legally considered "obscene." Police seized more than twenty thousand pounds of film that had been shipped in containers labeled "Donuts" and "Assorted Donuts." Meanwhile, Suffolk County District Attorney Garrett Byrne targeted Good Time Charlie's and the 663 Lounge on charges of allowing prostitution on the premises. Boston's entertainment licensing board stepped up action. In 1976, the licensing board received a total of 444 Combat Zone related complaints; 120 came during the last two months, after Puopolo's death. In the first half of 1977, the board received and acted on nearly five hundred.

Over the next ten years, Boston licensing officials set their sights on the clubs. Clubs either had their liquor licenses temporarily yanked by the Alcoholic Beverage Control Commission or their entertainment licenses suspended by the Boston Licensing Board. Pick your poison, officials were saying: either no booze or no broads. Both Consumer Affairs and Licensing Commissioner Diane Modica and Andrea Gargiulo, chair of the Boston Licensing Board, were kept busy fielding complaints about noise, fighting, prostitution, drugs, failing to maintain order, and even double-parking. Modica was constantly frustrated by businesses that hid behind the First Amendment or managers who professed not to know what one bartender did, or who was even working a shift on any given night. "We had to grant a license unless we found a public safety reason to deny the license," she said.

Combat Zone business owners shrugged. After all, it was what they expected. But Debra Beckerman was fed up. In 1977, she vanished from Boston. At one point her husband reported her as missing, but there were reports she was working in Montreal as a dancer using the name Silver Smith. In 1978, her former boyfriend, Jack Kelly, was found murdered, along with four others at the Blackfriars Pub near Downtown Crossing. The crime was never officially solved. BRA director Robert Kenney was gone by early 1977, and John Sloan was promoted to the prestigious post of director of urban design in 1978. He left the agency in 1980 following a clash with Mayor White over the development of Long Wharf in Boston.

Two years after Puopolo's death, the Combat Zone and Park Square still supported thirty-nine adult businesses, including clubs, peep shows, bookstores, and X-rated movies. Newsreels from 1977 to 1979 show the AED was as raunchy as ever. Despite Sloan's efforts, most of the signage along Washington Street had all the sophistication of those nude female silhouettes emblazoned on tire flaps. A bold brunette donning tiny pasties and a G-string glowered from the garish marquee of the Intermission Lounge. Next door, The Scene promised XXX adult movies for twenty-five cents. In bookstores, the brown paper wrappings had come off. A Combat Zone storefront window was filled with scintillating books like *The Blue-eyed Stud* and *Lisa's Adulterous Revenge*, and sex toys were on display nearby. Pedestrians passed with barely a glance at the now familiar streetscape of sleaze.

Clubs and bookstores continued to open and close in an erotic merry-go-round. The first major casualty was the "world famous" Two O'Clock Lounge, which had been socked with a series of entertainment and liquor license violations, in addition to charges of prostitution on the premises. The club finally shuttered in 1978. Within a year, the space was reborn as Disco 7, an all-night "juice bar," which attempted to evade liquor regulations by supposedly not serving alcohol. Such juice bars were not, according to *Globe* reporter Alan Richman, "to be confused with establishments specializing in citrus products. The only thing you can get fresh-squeezed is your head."

The Naked i upgraded its signage, going full neon with its infamous logo: a glowing eye smack dab between two upside-down legs, which now swayed hypnotically back and forth. Club 66 eventually squeezed next to the Naked i, at 662 Washington, and Liberty Book II, an "Adult Entertainment Complex," opened at 640-644 Washington Street. The Carnival at 39 Boylston became the Casino 39. The Club Baths, a gay bathhouse, was established in the upper floors of the Hayden Building, which had a roof deck for nude sunbathing.

The Pilgrim Theater carried on, showing X-rated films all night or nearly all night. Both the Pilgrim and the State Theater were known as gay cruising spots, where men would hook up for sexual romps in the bathroom. What seems soulless, unwise, and dangerous in today's era served as a refuge for many gay men. "These places existed not only so that men could watch the films but so that men could meet one another—socially and sexually. They were community meeting places," writes Michael Bronski in a collection of gay erotica. For many gay men, public sex was an expression of their identity. "Over the years, I've come to see the Pilgrim Theater as the zenith in the constellation of my cruising for hot public sex; a singular oasis in a city notable for its sexually repressed attitudes, even—surprisingly—within the gay community," Christopher Wittke writes in the collection.

The movie theaters and law enforcement engaged in a kind of legal tango over what constituted obscenity. Veteran Boston detective Edward McNelley describes the dance:

> You would have to go to into the movie theater and view the film. You'd have to write a play-by-play description. Unfortunately, the movies theaters were dark and you're trying to write and people are looking at you. Then we brought tape recorders and then they thought you were a real pervert talking to yourself. Then you would execute a search warrant that included the play by play. You would go up to court and they would issue you a search warrant. And you could go in and seize one copy of, say, *Deep Throat*. They would have ten more. You wouldn't be out the door and they would be playing it again. Then you have to set up for a hearing so we would have to rent a place to show the film and the judge along with the

clerks and the cops and the defense lawyer would go down there to view the film. If the judge determined it was (obscene), they would issue a complaint and have the arraignment and then have to go to a trial and go through the same thing again.

Indeed, McNelley is unsure if a single obscene film case was ever concluded.

Despite the increasing pressure, Combat Zone bars led something of a charmed existence. In February 1979, *Globe* reporter Richman systematically visited all eleven Combat Zone and Park Square strip clubs, carefully rating them with one to three cocktail glasses. At the Silver Slipper (two glasses), "the busty, overweight collection of strippers has been recruited more for mingling than dancing." Meanwhile, the Mousetrap (one glass) "at first glance looks like all the vinyl barstools have been in knife fights." Picc-a-dilly (two glasses) is all "glitter and hustle, nice looking but hard around the edges," while at the Caribe Lounge (three glasses), he watched a dancer perform "a floor act featuring a plastic squeeze bottle of body lotion." As for the strippers at the Intermission Lounge (one glass), "I would bet a couple of them taught Ann Corio how to dance."

By the late 1970s, the BRA was still scrambling to figure out how to revitalize Park Square, and now the agency was also looking at ways to jump-start theater renovations downtown. In 1979, the BRA issued a Theater and Entertainment District Report. Its portrait of the Combat Zone was as somber as the 1974 report was "gay and frisky." It included opinions from numerous constituencies. "The Zone polices itself," one interviewee said. "It's dirty, immoral, and more of a nuisance and embarrassment than anything." A police officer tellingly observed, "When they put in the Zone, they created what someone has called 'an illusion of license'—telling people that they are free to do what they want there."

For Chinatown residents, the AED had become an urban nightmare. Although many had acquiesced during the establishment of the AED, more were now seething. Unlike conventioneers who merely visited the Zone, Chinatown residents had to pass through blocks of pornographic stores, peep shows, and strip clubs as they went about their daily lives. The community was ready to be recognized as a neighborhood in the pantheon of Boston's power circles. Frank Chin knew that voting was the key; with votes came clout. Born in Chinatown, orphaned, and raised in China before returning to Boston, Frank Chin, known as "Uncle Frank," worked as a purchasing agent for three Boston mayors: White, Flynn, and Menino. A leader in the community, he began going door to door in the 1970s to register voters. By 1975, he had increased Chinatown's registered voters from about three hundred to thirty-six hundred. He was among those who initially thought Chinatown and the Combat Zone could coexist. "In the early days, the Combat Zone was more or less burlesque. They didn't have nudity," he said. "There were no drugs. Later on, there were drugs and houses of prostitution. It was bad. It hurt the business of Chinatown. People didn't want to go to Chinatown."

By the early 1980s, Chinatown leaders were actively calling for the elimination of the Combat Zone. Residents were organizing protests and midnight patrols, attempting to ward off hookers and dealers with cameras and flashlights. They complained that Boston had used their neighborhood as a dumping ground and now planned to increase property values to drive off adult businesses, which would also drive out low-income Chinese.

Boston's erogenous zone model lost favor. William Toner, a city planning consultant, told the *Wall Street Journal*, "Nobody wants to be known as the councilman who helped set up Pornography City." The era of porno chic was over, and even organized crime had moved into producing masturbatory fantasies for the new and growing videocassette market. Indeed, authors Eric Schaefer and Eithne Johnson argue the AED's problems helped re-stigmatize adult entertainment as it verged on legitimacy.

BRA officials continued to play the long game. For urban planners looking to sanitize the sullied reputation of Boston's downtown, hope finally came in the long-debated Park Square redevelopment. Early in the 1980s, the Park Square area was developed for the state transportation building, a process that evicted the fabled Hillbilly Ranch. The historic but rundown Statler Hotel was reborn as the Boston Park Plaza Hotel, and the luxury Four Seasons hotel, with equally lavish condos, was built on the former site of the Mousetrap, Teddy Bear Lounge, and Playboy Club, which had closed in 1977, on Boylston.

Chinatown organizes against the Combat Zone. Chinese Progressive Association records (M163), Archives and Special Collections Department, Northeastern University Libraries.

Despite the "Massachusetts Miracle" of the early 1980s, the longed-for economic development only came in fits and starts and had not truly reached the downtown. The BRA's 1979 report gloomily concluded, "There is no evidence that the businesses in the adult entertainment district are going to wither away and die." Yet something had to be done. The *Boston Globe,* which supported the creation of the AED, admitted as much in an editorial: "What is not at all clear is what should be done about the zone."

The dark side of the Zone.
©Jerry Berndt Estate.

CHAPTER 12

MOBSTERS IN THE ZONE

1977 to 1992

....

Those joints were all controlled by the wise guys.

BOSTON POLICE DETECTIVE BILLY DWYER

In 1983, the Combat Zone was definitely shrinking, but you'd never guess that from the inside of what Regina Quinlan called the Porno Palace—otherwise known as the Liberty Book Shop on Washington Street. That's where Steven Nichols would check in when he started his shift; he would either work there or be dispatched to another shop, such as the First Amendment Ltd., First Amendment II, or the Book Mart, all owned by the same guy—Mr. Palladino. No one crossed Mr. Palladino, who was known to explode into profanity at the drop of a hat. Nichols didn't ask questions, mostly because he didn't have to. Everyone knew Palladino answered to the Angiulo family of the North End, Boston's mob bosses at the time.

Nichols would tend the counter, ringing up the erotic books, magazines, and various sex toys, and sell tokens for the peep booths. He knew all the girls who worked there. They weren't hookers, not really, or at least not all of them. They were just attractive girls—and a few drag queens—who either wanted or needed the kind of money to be made by taking off their clothes and striking "erotic" poses. There was something called the carousel, even though the carousel didn't turn anymore because the device had broken down and the management hadn't bothered to get it fixed. Still, the girls would dutifully take their shifts on the stationary mechanism while men, who had purchased tokens for the adjoining booths, watched them writhe in simulated ecstasy. On most days, Nichols would walk back into the carousel and take the girls' orders for lunch.

For the most part, the job was a cakewalk. All he had to do was keep his mouth shut and he could earn three to four hundred dollars a week under the table. It was a damn fortune. As a gay man living in Boston in the 1980s, Nichols knew how to keep his mouth shut.

One summer Saturday, when he was finishing up his shift at midnight, another employee asked him if he could stay a bit and help out with tallying the take. Nichols obligingly went into the office of the Liberty Book Shop. "I never saw so much money in my life," he recalls. The desk was covered in stacks and stacks of cash. He started counting the bills—apparently just that week's income—trying not to think too much about where the money had come from and where it was going. He estimated there was about $150,000 in cash. "I was there until two o'clock in the morning counting." Was he tempted to put any in his pocket? Not on his life.

◆

It's not surprising that the mob controlled interests in the Combat Zone. It would be surprising if they didn't. "Back in the day, if there was a buck to be made, then there was organized crime," as a Boston police officer put it. Just how many places were owned and run by wise guys is, by the very nature of organized crime, a matter of conjecture and conflicting witness testimony. John Sloan, the architect, still remains unconvinced that mobsters "ran" the Zone; the place was too disorganized, he said. Yet two names pop up with regularity: Palladino and Venios.

Joseph N. Palladino and Anthony C. Russo of Winchester were associated with a number of bookstores in the Zone, including the Book Mart, The Scene, First Amendment Ltd., and the Liberty Book Shop. Palladino reportedly had interests in other New England bookstores, as well. Both he and Thomas Palladino, described by the FBI as his

Courtesy City of Boston.

cousin, were known associates of Gennaro "Jerry" Angiulo, the head of the Angiulo crime family. A confidential organized crime chart assembled by the Suffolk County District Attorney's Office in 1976 found that the Palladinos answered to the Angiulos, and the Angiulos to New England mafia boss Raymond Patriarcha, who answered to the New York families. Everyone knew this. But no one could prove it.

Teddy, Arthur, and Louis Venios, three Greek brothers from Woburn, were other well-known mobsters of the time. Even before they got tangled up in the Zone, the Venios brothers had long rap sheets, including arrests and sentences for fraud, swindles, illegal gambling, and schemes to distribute obscene material. Teddy Venios, known as "Teddy Venus," was, like Palladino, connected with the Angiulos. FBI wiretaps caught Angiulo ordering Louis Venios to "hit" his own son-in-law, Walter LaFreniere. LaFreniere, who was married to Venios' daughter, Helen, had run up a debt in a dice game run by the Angiulos. Those wires also caught Angiulo, Palladino, and others wrangling over profits from various sex-related businesses.

At one point in time, under the umbrella of an enterprise called Bel-Art Realty, the Venios brothers owned or had some ownership stake in the Two O'Clock Lounge, the Naked i, the Capri Cinema, the Mousetrap, the Twin-X Cinema, and four adult book and novelty shops. Not that this was clear from the paper trail. As the *Boston*

Phoenix reported, "Teddy is clearly the man who makes the decisions at the 'World Famous' Two O'Clock," but city records list the names of relatives or other acquaintances as the controlling corporation's president, treasurer, and shareholder. In fact, many Combat Zone businesses hid behind straw men. One "owner" had the Brahmin name of Theodore A. Pettypiece. According to Boston police veteran Ed McNelley, a couple of vice squad detectives spent three years tracking down Pettypiece. A man with that name was found living in Alaska and had apparently obligingly signed papers for a couple hundred dollars a year.

Sex-related businesses became increasingly attractive to wise guys after 1972. The establishment of the Massachusetts State Lottery took a big chunk out of the mob's most lucrative industry: playing the numbers. And if people weren't running up gambling debts or putting everything on a credit card, they had no need of loan sharks, another mob mainstay. Porn and strip clubs were looking like a good investment for the underworld. That was the meaty, legitimate part of the business, and for some club owners, the sideline business of prostitution and drug dealing was the gravy.

When Suffolk Country District Attorney Garrett Byrne got wind of prostitution in the Zone's clubs—with customers even paying for sex acts on credit cards—he joined the long list of people who would attempt to wipe out the Combat Zone. He took the proliferation of pornography personally, grousing to a *Herald American* reporter that high school boys were viewing porn films in the Zone. "Perhaps these smut peddlers are growing bolder because they have been encouraged by talk of the Liberty Tree Park." To lead the charge against immorality, Byrne enlisted the help of a young district attorney who joined his office in 1972.

Thomas E. Dwyer Jr. was less worried about naked women and more concerned about prostitution and organized crime. He pondered his legal options and decided to go after the clubs' liquor licenses. This would hit them where it hurt and it might force them into bankruptcy. To yank a license, he needed a reason. So, he targeted clubs presenting false information on just who owned them.

Working with Police Superintendent John Doyle, Dwyer put together an undercover team of young police officers unknown to the club owners to investigate the premises. The team's report provides a glimpse into the prostitution happening at places such as the Teddy

Bear Lounge, the Picc-a-dilly Club, and the Mousetrap. One investigator said a bartender told him that it "will only cost a hundred bucks" to spend a night with a performer. This particular investigator haggled the price to seventy dollars, then paid with a credit card. Investigators also reported that when they bought dancers seven-dollar drinks, the girls would obligingly expose themselves or fondle the men. In the eyes of the law, club owners were responsible for illegal acts occurring on their premises. The team's final report spanned hundreds of pages and was presented to Boston's licensing board in early 1975.

After the report was issued, Doyle took Dwyer on a visit to some of the places so he could see for himself what was going on. A man who demanded to know what they were doing there approached them. Doyle and Dwyer identified themselves and asked who the man was. "Well, this is my place. I own this place," the man retorted.

That was a bad move. Dwyer took him at his word. He filed suit against the man, George E. Tecci, for concealing his ownership in an entity called Number Three Lounge Inc.—which owned the Teddy Bear, Picc-a-dilly, and the Mousetrap—and for submitting liquor license transfers and license renewals under false names. In 1976, the State Alcoholic Beverage Control Commission permanently yanked the licenses for the Number Three Lounge clubs. The owners appealed, but in March 1979, an appeals court upheld the denial of licenses. In an effort to stay in business downtown, Tecci went on to operate the Teddy Bear Arcade with video and pinball games, but not for long.

The Venios brothers encountered similar troubles. According to case documents for *United States v. Bel-Art Realty*, from 1980 to 1986, Bel-Art Realty owned and operated a number of nightclubs, peep shows, movie theaters, and adult bookstores in Boston's Combat Zone but failed to disclose the identity and background of ownership to get proper licenses. "For good measure, between 1980 and 1986 [the defendants] bribed licensing board members and police officers to avoid accountability for infractions which might otherwise have resulted in license suspensions or revocations," court documents read. In 1989, Venios and two others were indicted on two Racketeer Influenced and Corrupt Organizations Act (RICO) counts and multiple mail fraud counts. They were found guilty in 1989, lost their appeal in 1992, and they were slapped with huge fines and prison sentences.

The connection between the mob and sex-related businesses was not unique to Boston. Around the country, organized crime dominated the traditional porn industry, as well as massage parlors, topless bars, and strip joints, according to *Time* magazine. The *Boston Globe*'s Spotlight investigative team reached the same conclusion.

Palladino operated bookstores through the early 2000s, but his ties to organized crime, as well as loud opposition by Chinatown residents, stymied his 1998 efforts to build what might have been the Zone's largest strip club above Liberty Book II on Washington Street. The property was eventually sold, along with the Naked i and the Pilgrim, to developer Kevin Fitzgerald.

Mark Pasquale, whose father ran the King of Pizza near Palladino's porn businesses, remembers Palladino as a shrewd businessman. "He was the king," Pasquale said. "Everything he did … was top notch. There were no cutting corners. Joe was like Donald Trump. He

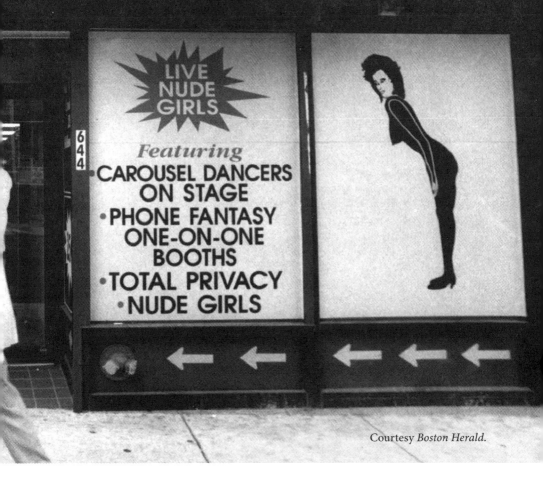

Courtesy *Boston Herald*.

only did the best of the best." Steve Nichols, the dirty bookstore clerk, remembers Palladino quite differently. Palladino eventually retired and has since passed on, Pasquale said.

Thomas Dwyer, who went on to a distinguished legal career, does not look back kindly on his Zone investigation days. "I think the Combat Zone was a cancer… and the DNA of that cancer was corruption. No Combat Zone could exist in the city of Boston without systemic corruption. So, when I look at it, all I see is corruption. I don't see anything else."

Steve Nichols quit the bookstore business in 1987 when he was accused falsely of dipping into the till; he went on to a career in the airline industry. "The job was not good; it was not bad. I look back at it now, and I realize if it hadn't been for the money I would not have lasted six months. Deep down, I didn't like it."

The Home of *Dickie-Blouse of*

Dickie-Blouse of Boston

PRODUCTS SOLD
IN LEADING STORES

PARKING
3 RIGHT TURNS TO
SHOPPERS GARAGE

CAFETERIA
Albiani

KING
OF
PIZZA

Coca-Cola

SHERMAN
WATCHES · DIAMONDS
JEWELRY
MONEY · LOAN

SHERMAN
WATCHES · DIAMONDS
JEWELRY
· LOAN

SHERMAN
WATCHES
MONEY · LOAN

Bottl
LIQUO
BOYLSTON WINE

WATCH REPAIRING

BOYLSTON WINE

TOW AREA
NO
PARKING
7 A.M. TO 6 P.M.
EXCEPT SUNDAYS

ONE WAY

CHAPTER 13

WITH A BANG AND A WHIMPER

1980 to 2016

....

Like a stripper who knows she's past her prime, the Combat Zone is retreating down the runway toward a curtain that is about to close on it forever. The Zone's obituary has been written before— based primarily on wishful thinking by politicians. But in recent months, major development has gained control of most of the property in Boston's adult entertainment district.

GEOFFREY ROWAN, *BOSTON HERALD*, APRIL 20, 1986

For fifteen years, King of Pizza owner "Tony King" Pasquale loved his work and his customers, whether cop or commuter, prostitute or pimp. So he was baffled when the King of Pizza was forced out of the Boylston Building in the early 1980s. He and Joe Palladino, who owned the adult bookstores there, tried to buy the building when it went up for sale but were outbid at the last moment. Both he and Palladino were told they would have to vacate. Pasquale took the offered relocation money but had no heart to open a new place. Devastated, he retired to the North End and his chapter in the Combat Zone was over. The Zone itself would follow him into retirement. After years of defying predictions, Boston's adult entertainment playground headed into oblivion, taking down clubs, bars, peep shows, bookstores, and a family-owned pizza joint.

The impending death of the Combat Zone was predicted for half as long as its existence. A BRA official insisted in 1977 that "for all intents and purposes, the Combat Zone is dead." On June 9, 1978, the *Christian Science Monitor* opined, "the Combat Zone has all but expired." On July 30, the *Boston Herald* was far more blunt: "The Combat Zone is dying." In 1980, Boston Mayor Kevin White predicted the Zone would be eliminated within thirty-six months. Eight years later in March of 1988, the end was again nigh, but the *Boston Globe* added a question mark: "The Final Chapter for the Zone?" Seven years later, on December 17, 1995, the *Globe* conceded, "The Combat Zone refuses to die."

What would finally spell doom for the Zone was something that 1970s planners never dreamed of: technology.

The long-hoped-for rise in Boston's downtown real estate value came slowly. In 1980, a spruced-up Liberty Tree Building was placed on the National Register of Historic Places, St. Francis House opened its doors on Boylston Street to serve the hapless, and Park Square finally got its facelift. There were now posh hotels, like the Four Seasons and the Boston Park Plaza Hotel, the Heritage on the Garden condos, and an influx of restaurants like Legal Sea Foods that all conspired to make Park Square once again a fashionable—and expensive—address. The Boylston Building was also placed on the register of historic places, but its upper floors, like that of the Liberty Tree Building, were largely vacant. Still, prices were trending upward. In 1981, office space in the Combat Zone sold for five to seven dollars per square foot. By 1984, the prices were up to nineteen dollars per square foot, although comparatively, prices elsewhere in downtown Boston were thirty to forty dollars per square foot.

Succeeding Mayor White in 1984 was a canny Boston politician cut from an entirely different cloth. Former state representative Raymond Flynn was a fervent and implacable foe of the adult entertainment district. Flynn had attended the September 11, 1974 zoning commission meeting and was surprised that more residents didn't speak up. "You would have thought they would bring the house down," he recalled. That lack of opposition to the Combat Zone profoundly affected the young legislator. "This will become the 'anything goes district,'" he warned. There was a "silence in the city from people who should have been more vocal and more visible. It kind of helped formulate my political [thought that] the only way for evil to prevail is for good people to do nothing."

Flynn vowed to eliminate the Zone once and for all, pledging to get tough on building code violations, prostitution, and drug trafficking. The year he took office, there were an estimated twenty-four to twenty-six strip clubs, bookstores, and movie houses in the area. However, developers such as the Bass Brothers, Allright Boston Parking, and Boston's largest residential landlord, Harold Brown, began to buy property there. In 1986, with the help of the BRA, the Chinese Economic Development Council took over the Boylston Building with plans to open the China Trade Center, a showcase for Asian market goods. Four pornographic bookstores, two strip clubs, and the King of Pizza were evicted. In the early 1990s, the China Trade Center went bankrupt and the BRA purchased the property in 1993, mainly to prevent it from being taken over again by adult entertainment.

In 1987, the Pussy Cat Lounge shut its doors, its owner citing a five-fold rent increase. The club's entire contents, including its runway and the orange and yellow Pussy Cat sign, were auctioned off. The owner of the building, David Wong, converted the space into Asian restaurants and renovated offices. Wong also owned the nearby Center Theatre and transformed it first into the Pagoda Theater and then into Empire Garden, a one thousand-seat dim sum restaurant and meeting place. The Pussycat Cinema next door became a McDonald's. In 1987, thirty new Asian businesses, many run by Vietnamese, opened in the area. By the end of that year, the number of strip joints had decreased to five. An unnamed city official told a *Boston Herald* reporter, "Even organized crime figures who have been linked to most parcels in the Zone can't make as much money selling drugs and managing prostitutes as they can selling the property to developers."

Rising real estate prices alone, however, couldn't take down the Zone. Some of the more profitable adult businesses could still afford the higher rents. But customers were drifting elsewhere, particularly to large "gentlemen's" clubs that had sprung up in the suburbs. More importantly, those seeking titillation didn't have to go anywhere. They could just stay home and pop a tape into the increasingly ubiquitous videocassette recorder.

Introduced to the United States around 1977, the VCR transformed the country's television watching habits. Some analysts even insist that pornography consumers were the driving force behind the VCR market. In 1980, there were fewer than two million VCRs in American households; by 1989, there were sixty-two million. "People willing to pay dearly for the ability to watch skin flicks from the comfort of their home helped keep the entire home video industry afloat long enough for the tech to mature and become affordable for the masses," *Digital Trends* reported. The February 1983 *Globe* Spotlight series on pornography concluded that there was no place like home for porn:

> Five years after the sale of the first home video machines, the marketing of hardcore cassettes through video stores has transformed the adult-film industry to the point of making it legitimate. Increasingly, the place to watch such films is not in a Combat Zone theater or peep show booth. It is in the home, on a television set connected to a video machine.

While Combat Zone bookstores initially made a killing selling X-rated videos, video tapes quickly became available in the "adults only" sections of local video stores. Cable TV and satellite networks eventually eliminated the need to run to the store.

"What basically happened is that people's technology changed. Morality changed. That's what killed the Combat Zone," Ed McNelley said. "At one point, you had to go there to get a dirty magazine. And now you can get on Amazon and order all you want. To watch a dirty movie you had to go there. Now you can use your clicker…"

The emergence of the Internet in the 1980s and the World Wide Web in 1989 closed the coffin lid. Craigslist and other online ad sites became more efficient vehicles for prostitution than streetwalking or "escort service" ads in the alternative newspapers. In the late 1970s, the vice squad would arrest up to 120 hookers on a weekend in the Zone. By 1989, eighty would be arrested per month.

The BRA continued to promulgate plans for revitalizing downtown. In late 1987, the agency issued a Midtown Cultural District Plan intended to increase housing for Chinatown, improve transportation access, and adapt historic preservation practices.

Elected in 1993, Thomas Menino would become Boston's longest serving mayor. Under his administration, the Combat Zone continued to shrink as his office worked to bring new businesses into Boston. However, major private investment in both upper and lower Washington Street remained problematic well into the 2010s. The city had great hopes for Lafayette Place, a retail development just off Washington Street that was built in 1984. It was, however, a business failure almost from the start. A decade later, there was an effort to build a massive mixed-use project on Washington Street near the Boston Common. But the plans for Commonwealth Center never got off the ground. In 1997, Millennium Partners, a large New York-based development firm, took over the site and launched a half-billion-dollar project to build the Ritz-Carlton's Boston Common hotel, 270 luxury condos, eighty-five extended-stay apartments, two restaurants and a lounge, a one-hundred-thousand-square-foot health club, fifty thousand square feet of retail space, and a nineteen-screen Loew's Theater complex. When Millennium Place opened in 2001, the complex was regarded as a gamble in what was still considered a dicey neighborhood. The gamble paid off: Millennium Place proved to be the anchor of a revitalized downtown.

In 1997, another important step was taken. The now vacant Liberty Tree Building got a surprising new tenant in the state's Registry of Motor Vehicles. It was a sign of confidence that the area was changing.

The Naked i hung on until the mid-1990s. When owner Mel Horowitz died, his son Jeffrey took over, but he didn't have his father's touch. At the time, the building was owned by developer and parking lot magnate Kevin Fitzgerald, who also owned the Liberty Tree Building. Fitzgerald wanted the land for parking lots or another kind of development. Horowitz was not able to open a club elsewhere. In April of 1996, the buildings housing both the Naked i and the Pilgrim Theater were gutted and torn down. Jeffrey Horowitz eventually sold the coveted operating license to Centerfolds, a chain of "gentlemen's clubs." In 2001, after numerous legal battles with the city, the chain opened a club in a vacant space at 12-18 LaGrange Street.

The iconic Naked i sign was saved by David Waller, that young Parker House doorman who always knew which way to point fellows looking for a little action. Waller became a video production specialist and sign collector; when he got wind that the Naked i building was

The Silver Slipper, reborn as the Glass Slipper, is one of the
two remaining strip clubs in the now-defunct Combat Zone.
Courtesy *Boston Herald*.

to be torn down, he won permission from developer Kevin Fitzgerald
to dismantle and haul away the thirty-foot-long Naked i marquee.
Later, he was able to purchase one of a pair of neon signs with the eye
and moving legs. The marquee is now on loan to West End Johnnie's,
a Boston bar and restaurant. The legs sign was loaned to a photography exhibit on the Combat Zone in 2010 but has remained in storage
since. "It's way beyond offensive, in bad taste, no question," Waller
said. Nonetheless, he considers it a part of Boston's history.

The Silver Slipper turned out to be a Cinderella story. Forced to close
when the Boylston Building was turned into the China Trade Center, it
eventually relocated to the corner of LaGrange and Washington Streets

and was reborn as the Glass Slipper. In 2004, that location and the nearby Publix Theater were taken by eminent domain for the Kensington, a luxury apartment project. Glass Slipper owner Nick Romano, a North End businessman, fiercely fought the eviction. "We weren't against the Glass Slipper per se," recalls the BRA's Paul McCann. "We were against curtailing the development of that block. Kensington had been able to acquire everything else around it. They were not able to acquire the Glass Slipper. They wouldn't even take his calls. They could offer him ten million dollars and he wouldn't take it. He just wanted to stay where they were." By law, the BRA had to find the business a new location, something McCann recalls with some glee. With relocation funds, McCann was able move the Glass Slipper across LaGrange to a location next to Centerfolds. "They can be there forever if they want it," he said.

Today, the Glass Slipper and Centerfolds are the only strip clubs operating in the Zone on a now sedate LaGrange Street. The last adult video and paraphernalia shop disappeared from the area in the summer of 2016.

Menino has been hailed as the mayor who finally brought the Combat Zone to heel. However, preservationists argued that the mayor's approach was "to destroy the village in order to save it," particularly with regard to the Zone's nineteenth and early twentieth century buildings. There was a concerted effort to save the Publix at 545 Washington, formerly the Gaiety Theatre, which was built in 1908 and closed since 1988. The Gaiety was one of the few places to host traveling shows featuring black performers such as Josephine Baker, Florence Mills, and Ethel Waters, and supporters pleaded for its preservation as part of the city's multicultural history. However, after a long fight, the structure was not granted landmark status by the Boston Landmark Commission. Following the outrage at the loss of the Gaiety, there were increased pressures to protect and revitalize the other historic theaters in the district. After decades of showing B-grade movies or sitting empty on Washington Street, the historic Paramount movie theater, the Opera House, and the Modern Theater were meticulously restored and reopened in projects mounted by Suffolk University, Emerson College, and other entities.

The five-story Hayden Building proved to be another win for preservationists. This commercial building at the corner of Washington and

LaGrange was built in the 1870s, after an explosion at a nearby drug store leveled the block. Over the decades, it hosted a number of business, including tailors, jewelers, a record store, an Army-Navy surplus store, and the LaGrange Health Club with sauna and steam baths. It eventually became the home for The Scene peep shows on the ground floor and the Club Baths, part of a chain of gay bath clubs, on the upper floors. In 1973, Cynthia Zaitzevsky published an article in the *Journal of the Society of Architectural Historians* about her discovery that the building was designed by famed architect Henry Hobson Richardson for his father-in-law, John C. Hayden. Richardson, who designed Boston's remarkable Trinity Church, is considered one of America's premiere builders. An architectural gem was housing dirty movies.

Unlike the Gaiety Theatre, this building was given landmark status. The Scene eventually folded, and a fire gutted the top floors in 1985. In 1993, Historic Boston, a nonprofit that saves and rehabilitates historic properties, formed a partnership with Chinese businessman and developer David Wong. They bought the building, probably for less than half a million dollars. The partners revamped the structure, creating new retail space on the first floor and eventually built out the apartments on the upper floors. Some amusing items were discovered during the remodel, including a list of what to do in case of a police raid: "Make a PA announcement" and "Stay calm." Today, artwork in the building's common areas are the only reminders to residents that they live in a former peep show parlor. An art installation featuring strips of pornographic film, rescued from the dumpster across the street, was eventually removed due to complaints from the new residents.

Heeding the lessons of Scollay Square, it would be foolish to think that the businesses of the Combat Zone have vanished. They have simply morphed and moved elsewhere—to Craigslist, the Playboy Channel, and porn websites. At the Four Seasons Hotel, which replaced the Mousetrap and the Teddy Bear Lounge, guests can order and watch X-rated movies in their rooms as easily as grabbing a drink from the minibar.

Boston no longer needs a Combat Zone.

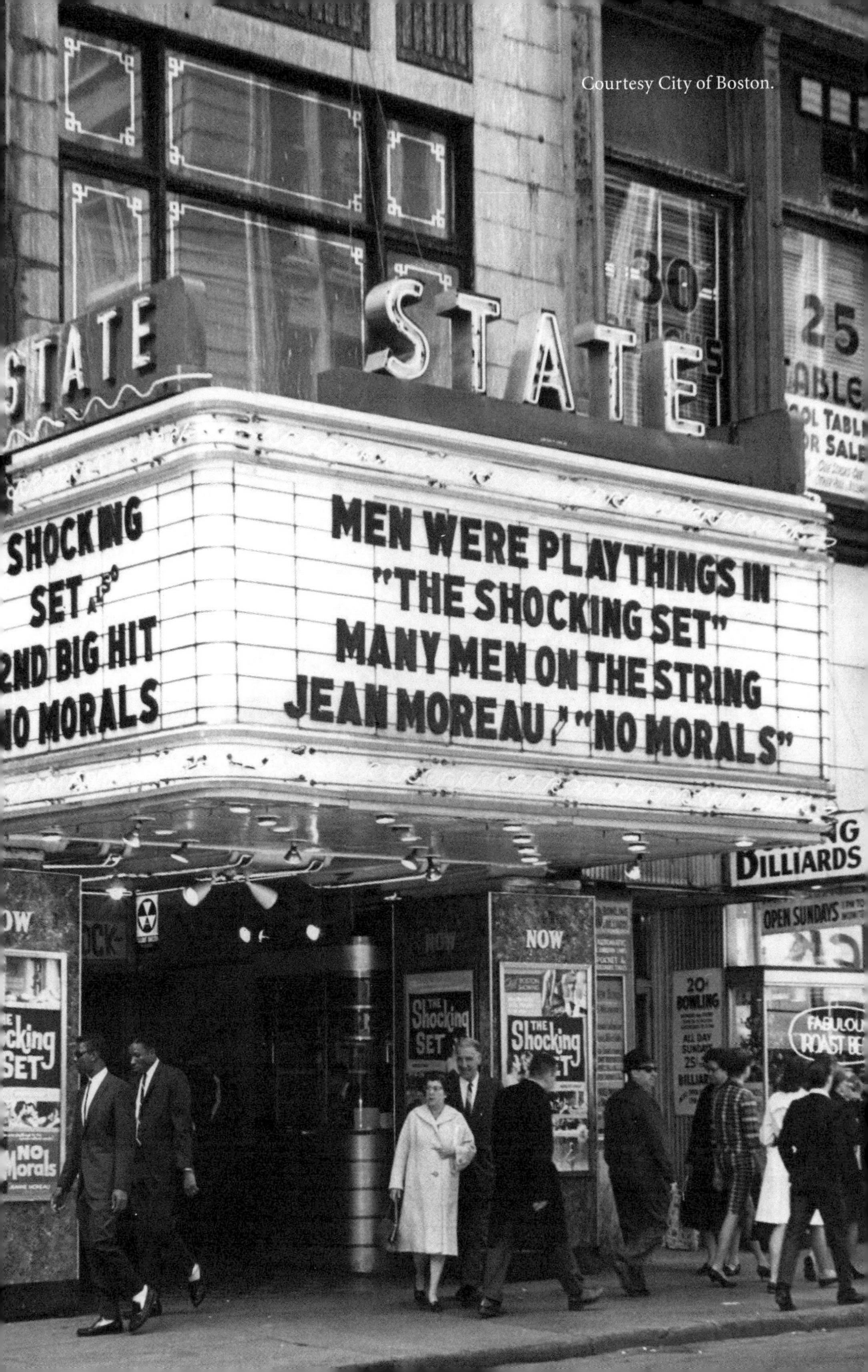

Courtesy City of Boston.

CHAPTER 14

SAYING GOODBYE TO THE ZONE

....

If you got rid of the Combat Zone, you'd probably create just another Yuppie enclave. Do we really need more of those?

WILLIAM CONDO, THEATER DISTRICT PROJECT DIRECTOR,
BOSTON REDEVELOPMENT AUTHORITY, DECEMBER 28, 1984

Walking through what used to be the Combat Zone, Mark Pasquale pointed toward an upscale restaurant on Washington Street. "That was the Two O'Clock." His finger drifted. "That was the Pilgrim Theater. Next door, that was the Naked i." He turned the corner at Boylston Street, going past the former location of his father's pizza place in the Boylston Building. "Here was the Silver Slipper. Here used to be a little variety store. And then you had the pornography shops all along here." He walked a bit further. "Here's where Andrew Puopolo was killed." Retracing his steps back to Washington, past Liberty Tree Park, he stopped near an Asian restaurant. "That was the Pussy Cat Lounge. That whole corner." He looked up at the beige and gray walls of the Kensington luxury apartment building at the corner of Washington and LaGrange, where a studio apartment goes for $4,620 a month. "I'd like to know who's paying that rent," he said, shaking his head. He looked down, amused by the worn, grimy brick below his feet. "The sidewalks haven't changed. They look the same." How does coming back here make him feel?

"We should have bought more property," he said glumly.

In February 2010, the legs of the Naked i Cabaret began to move again. The neon sign with its shrewdly placed eye lit up Harrison Avenue in Boston as part of an exhibit at the Howard Yezerski Gallery. "Boston: Combat Zone 1967-1978" featured images from three photographers who captured the Zone in its heyday: Roswell Angier, Jerry Berndt, and John Goodman. The exhibit triggered an outpouring of stories about the "old Combat Zone," a mixture of nostalgia and "good riddance." A neighborhood that had died a long, tortured death was briefly resurrected. Princess Cheyenne herself dropped by, insisting that the moody, dark photos did not match her memories of a vibrant, colorful time.

Like the patterns of a kaleidoscope that changes with every twist, Bostonians each see the Zone differently.

Former Miss Bicentennial Julie Jordan remembers her Combat Zone days with great affection. "I love that I got to be part of a piece of history; a world that will never exist again. It was a counterculture. It was a world where misfits fit in. It was a world of people who went against the norm and felt at home there. It was a community unto itself."

Thirty years after he left the Combat Zone and became a successful West Coast architect, Jonathan Tudan published a memoir called *Lovers, Muggers & Thieves*, committing to print stories that he had told friends for years. "I don't look back nostalgically; I don't," he recalls. "The streets were dirty, the clubs were dirty, filthy. I didn't like living like that. All the women [the dancers] wanted to be somewhere else. Their choices in life were limited."

While the Combat Zone strippers interviewed for this book acknowledged the unhealthy aspects of their lifestyles, none regret the experience. Theirs is not, however, a representative sample of dancers. They are the ones who survived without falling into drugs or turning tricks, who lived well enough to answer questions from an inquiring writer. "It is important to note that different participants experienced the Zone in very different ways, and that traditional power relationships did not disappear when one stepped across its border," dance professor Jessica Berson writes. "Many women working in the Zone were subjected to dehumanizing working conditions and constant harassment, and there are numerous stories of women abused by pimps, club managers, bouncers, and customers." At the same time, however, she believes the Combat Zone allowed for explorations of sexuality, gender, and desire discouraged in the rest of the city.

Outright prostitution, even under the guise of consenting adults, hardly merits nostalgia. Yet it's hard not to feel something for the elderly man who called himself "Brother Ralph," who spoke with affection of a Combat Zone hooker he used to visit. "She became a close friend. I got to meet a lot of her family. We became really good friends. It's strange but that's what happened," he said. On her sixtieth birthday, Ralph called and left a message to wish her happy birthday. She called back to marvel that he remembered.

Angel "Satan's Angel" Walker hung up the G-string in 1985, but at seventy-two years old, she still does occasional shows and teaches burlesque classes, including tassel twirling, near her Palm Springs, California, home. "I gave my whole life to burlesque," she says. "I bet I must have worked fifty times in Boston. I never saved a dime. But I looked good. I had a great apartment. I had a brand new Lincoln. Where's all that shit now? It's all gone."

Tucked away on LaGrange, the Glass Slipper and Centerfolds endure. Dancers at the Glass Slipper on an afternoon look worn and overweight, doing their best despite an aura of been there, bumped that. At Centerfolds, "dancing" is largely writhing on the stage floor and squirming against the center stage pole. There's very little tease in the strip. The girls remove a piece of clothing with each piped-in song: a cover up that's more shower curtain than negligee, a bra, and the G-string. They carefully hang each piece on a hook at the rear of the stage. Men whoop and holler and toss money at them; they also watch the Red Sox, Patriots, or Celtics on the two large flat screen TVs that flank the stage. Not even the sight of naked girls keeps patrons from checking their cell phones. When their act is finally done, the women crawl on hands and knees to sweep up the bills, carefully put on their "clothing," and, clutching the bills, slip upstairs. The next girl comes on and begins the routine by wiping down the pole and stairway handrails. Hygienic, yes. Erotic, not so much.

Strangely enough, burlesque—or what's regarded as neo-burlesque—has made a comeback with a distinct feminist twist. Troupes like Rogue Burlesque and Boston BeauTease regularly stage shows in which women of all shapes and ages perform burlesque routines, stripping down to pasties and G-strings. With a focus on creative character development, storytelling, glamour, and body positivity, these women (and a few men) are taking to the stage to express themselves in a whole new way. "Dedicated to recreating a Golden Age of Burlesque that never really existed," local performers like Brandy Wine, Betty Blaize, and Devora Darling revive the rhinestones and feathers in campy, bawdy shows in theaters, bars, and even YMCAs. It's certainly a different way of looking at cultural history.

Boston is a historical city proud of its landmarks, whether it be the Freedom Trail, the CITGO sign in Kenmore Square, or the memory of Scollay Square. For better or worse, the Combat Zone is part of that history. "It died a natural death with that kind of material being more accessible in a changing culture," said Regina Quinlan, the nun turned First Amendment lawyer. The assassin that led to the Combat Zone's demise has also met its end. In July of 2016, the last manufacturer of the home-use video cassette recorder announced it was ending production.

Those who opposed the creation of the AED—Ray Flynn, the police, and others—remain convinced it was a mistake. "Just ask the Puopolo family," one critic remarked. Architect John Sloan disagrees. "All you have to do is look at other cities; the question is proliferation. If you wanted to stop proliferation, this was the best alternative." Former congressman Barney Frank, who still insists the Combat Zone was born from Boston's excessive puritanical attitudes about sex among consenting adults, said the lesson of the AED is "a recognition that you can't control that kind of behavior and that you shouldn't try on any grounds other than nuisance."

Paul McCann, who retired in 2005, believes the Combat Zone worked exactly as intended. Look at the area now, he says. "It did everything we hoped it would … We protected the city from having Combat Zone uses in every area. It controlled adult entertainment in a day when it was out of control." In September 2016, under the new administration of Mayor Marty Walsh, the Boston Redevelopment Authority got an updated mission and a new name: the Boston Planning and Development Agency (BPDA).

Downtown Boston now has its high spine: high-rises line the area around Washington Street. The peak is the sixtieth floor of the residential skyscraper Millennial Tower, built on top of the famed Filene's building on upper Washington Street. The skyscrapers, luxury condos, trendy coffee shops, and hip restaurants are a better fit for a city than the Naked i or the Liberty Book Shop. Somehow, however, much of Washington Street's landscape seems bland and bloodless, another urban street in another city. Chinatown, however, retains much of its character, and Asian businesses have spread. Many Bostonians like to say that the Combat Zone *is* Chinatown now.

The Internet has resurrected its memories, some softened by time. When editor Adam Gaffin set up a comment thread about the Combat Zone on his Boston news site, Universal Hub, the electronic podium was flooded:

"I spent some of my finest hours at the Pilgrim Theater sneaking in cans of Schlitz and drooling over the strippers."

"I used to go to the Naked Eye [sic] all the time. I still remember the first time someone brought me there in the late 70's. It was a shocking, joyous feeling to walk in off the street and see two naked women at opposite ends of the long bar."

"The ambience of the whole Combat Zone on a Friday or Saturday night was electrifying to a young kid having his first experience in such an area."

The thread is not just for men and their tales from the vortex. A stripper called Panama Red fondly recalls fellow dancer Machine Gun Kelly. Another performer, Tangerine, pours out her entire life story, including working for Teddy Venus and dancing at the Pussy Cat Lounge. A woman who went by Fern Rivendrop describes dancing at the Naked i during the early- to mid-1980s. "My first shift ... ended ... when Princess Cheyenne came out on stage and danced her way through a set of Genesis, Kim Carnes, and Cat Stevens. Watching her twirl in a long, flowing blue cape under the black lights, to the song, 'She's Got Bette Davis Eyes,' I knew that I wanted to reach her level of skill, if not status."

Another dancer, CeeJay, writes: "This is where I really grew up and learned many lessons which actually have benefitted me in career today. Looking back is like watching a movie, so many lives ago."

For all its tarnished glitz, mob connections, and seamy sexual transactions, the Combat Zone was also a place where people worked, lived, and found community. The Universal Hub comments, woven together, create a tapestry of recollections and reveal the pull of the past, the joy of a wild youth in the rearview mirror, and a vision of Boston gone forever.

What isn't gone is the zoning amendment that created the adult entertainment district. It remains on the books.

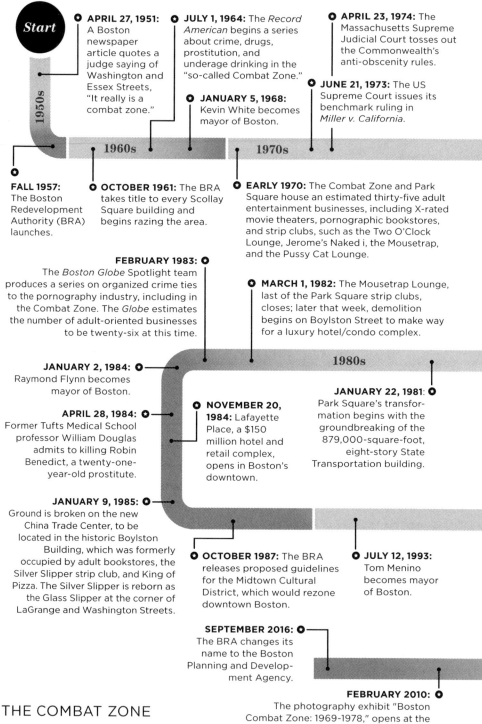

Start

APRIL 27, 1951: A Boston newspaper article quotes a judge saying of Washington and Essex Streets, "It really is a combat zone."

JULY 1, 1964: The *Record American* begins a series about crime, drugs, prostitution, and underage drinking in the "so-called Combat Zone."

JANUARY 5, 1968: Kevin White becomes mayor of Boston.

APRIL 23, 1974: The Massachusetts Supreme Judicial Court tosses out the Commonwealth's anti-obscenity rules.

JUNE 21, 1973: The US Supreme Court issues its benchmark ruling in *Miller v. California.*

1950s

1960s

1970s

FALL 1957: The Boston Redevelopment Authority (BRA) launches.

OCTOBER 1961: The BRA takes title to every Scollay Square building and begins razing the area.

EARLY 1970: The Combat Zone and Park Square house an estimated thirty-five adult entertainment businesses, including X-rated movie theaters, pornographic bookstores, and strip clubs, such as the Two O'Clock Lounge, Jerome's Naked i, the Mousetrap, and the Pussy Cat Lounge.

FEBRUARY 1983: The *Boston Globe* Spotlight team produces a series on organized crime ties to the pornography industry, including in the Combat Zone. The *Globe* estimates the number of adult-oriented businesses to be twenty-six at this time.

MARCH 1, 1982: The Mousetrap Lounge, last of the Park Square strip clubs, closes; later that week, demolition begins on Boylston Street to make way for a luxury hotel/condo complex.

1980s

JANUARY 2, 1984: Raymond Flynn becomes mayor of Boston.

APRIL 28, 1984: Former Tufts Medical School professor William Douglas admits to killing Robin Benedict, a twenty-one-year-old prostitute.

NOVEMBER 20, 1984: Lafayette Place, a $150 million hotel and retail complex, opens in Boston's downtown.

JANUARY 22, 1981: Park Square's transformation begins with the groundbreaking of the 879,000-square-foot, eight-story State Transportation building.

JANUARY 9, 1985: Ground is broken on the new China Trade Center, to be located in the historic Boylston Building, which was formerly occupied by adult bookstores, the Silver Slipper strip club, and King of Pizza. The Silver Slipper is reborn as the Glass Slipper at the corner of LaGrange and Washington Streets.

OCTOBER 1987: The BRA releases proposed guidelines for the Midtown Cultural District, which would rezone downtown Boston.

JULY 12, 1993: Tom Menino becomes mayor of Boston.

SEPTEMBER 2016: The BRA changes its name to the Boston Planning and Development Agency.

FEBRUARY 2010: The photography exhibit "Boston Combat Zone: 1969-1978," opens at the Howard Yezerski Gallery. The neon legs

THE COMBAT ZONE
TIMELINE

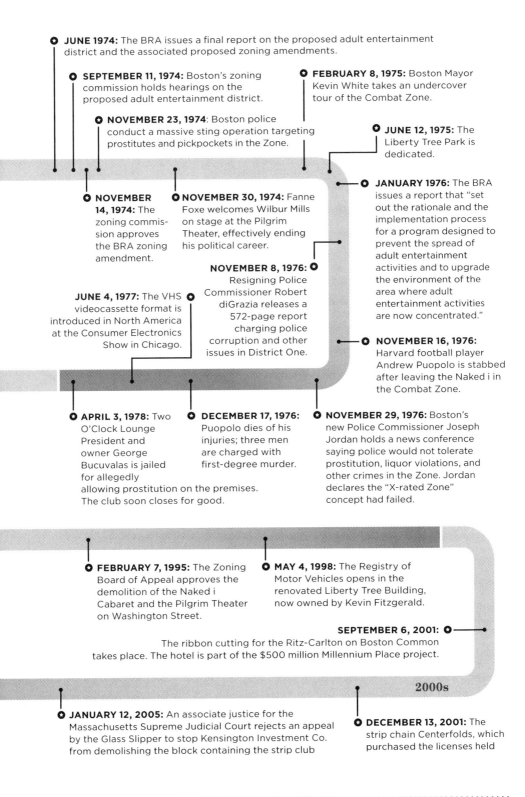

JUNE 1974: The BRA issues a final report on the proposed adult entertainment district and the associated proposed zoning amendments.

SEPTEMBER 11, 1974: Boston's zoning commission holds hearings on the proposed adult entertainment district.

FEBRUARY 8, 1975: Boston Mayor Kevin White takes an undercover tour of the Combat Zone.

NOVEMBER 23, 1974: Boston police conduct a massive sting operation targeting prostitutes and pickpockets in the Zone.

JUNE 12, 1975: The Liberty Tree Park is dedicated.

NOVEMBER 14, 1974: The zoning commission approves the BRA zoning amendment.

NOVEMBER 30, 1974: Fanne Foxe welcomes Wilbur Mills on stage at the Pilgrim Theater, effectively ending his political career.

JANUARY 1976: The BRA issues a report that "set out the rationale and the implementation process for a program designed to prevent the spread of adult entertainment activities and to upgrade the environment of the area where adult entertainment activities are now concentrated."

NOVEMBER 8, 1976: Resigning Police Commissioner Robert diGrazia releases a 572-page report charging police corruption and other issues in District One.

JUNE 4, 1977: The VHS videocassette format is introduced in North America at the Consumer Electronics Show in Chicago.

NOVEMBER 16, 1976: Harvard football player Andrew Puopolo is stabbed after leaving the Naked i in the Combat Zone.

APRIL 3, 1978: Two O'Clock Lounge President and owner George Bucuvalas is jailed for allegedly allowing prostitution on the premises. The club soon closes for good.

DECEMBER 17, 1976: Puopolo dies of his injuries; three men are charged with first-degree murder.

NOVEMBER 29, 1976: Boston's new Police Commissioner Joseph Jordan holds a news conference saying police would not tolerate prostitution, liquor violations, and other crimes in the Zone. Jordan declares the "X-rated Zone" concept had failed.

FEBRUARY 7, 1995: The Zoning Board of Appeal approves the demolition of the Naked i Cabaret and the Pilgrim Theater on Washington Street.

MAY 4, 1998: The Registry of Motor Vehicles opens in the renovated Liberty Tree Building, now owned by Kevin Fitzgerald.

SEPTEMBER 6, 2001: The ribbon cutting for the Ritz-Carlton on Boston Common takes place. The hotel is part of the $500 million Millennium Place project.

2000s

JANUARY 12, 2005: An associate justice for the Massachusetts Supreme Judicial Court rejects an appeal by the Glass Slipper to stop Kensington Investment Co. from demolishing the block containing the strip club

DECEMBER 13, 2001: The strip chain Centerfolds, which purchased the licenses held

ACKNOWLEDGMENTS

A book such as this would not be possible without assistance, advice, and encouragement from a huge number of people—a few of whom asked to remain anonymous. I am eternally grateful to the many researchers, retired officials, academics, journalists, former musicians, and library staffers who patiently answered my inquiries as well as the many folks who responded to my questions posted on Facebook.

I am especially thankful to Jessica Berson, Jan Brogan, and David Kruh for sharing their research. I want to very much thank for their time and insights: Paul McCann, Regina Quinlan, Mark Pasquale, John Sloan, Barney Frank, Mr. and Mrs. Ray Flynn, Kevin Fitzgerald, Thomas Dwyer, George Mansour, Diane Modica, Lauri Umansky, Julie Jordan, Steve Nichols, Elizabeth Brawner, Jonathan Tudan, Joel Feingold, Lisa Treat, Heidi Pangratis, Peter Chan, "Uncle Frank" Chin and his sister Amy, Angel Walker, Howard Yezerski, Peter Bates, and others who asked not to be named. Very special gratitude goes to law enforcement experts Billy Dwyer and Ed McNelley for sharing their recollections. Very deep thanks go to Danny Puopolo and Francesca Sciaba for reliving a nightmare for me. I sincerely thank Marta Crilly, Margaret Sullivan, Rosemarie Sansone, Don Stradley, Tom Palmer, Stephen Kurkjian, Judy Rakowsky, Martha Stone, Mark Krone, Nathaniel Sheidley, Lisa Tuite, Renee DeKona, Susan Chinsen, David Bernstein, and Carol Rosenberg for their assistance, stories, referrals, suggestions, and support. Kathy Kottaridis and the staff of Historic Boston must be acknowledged for giving me a tour of the Hayden Building and regaling me with stories about its rehabilitation.

Everlasting gratitude goes to Arthur Pollock, *Boston Herald* photographer extraordinaire, for his service, encouragement, and stories. (Also for the bagels). A shout-out to Donna Halper for finding a key article for me, and to David Waller for rescuing the Naked i marquee. I am extremely appreciative of Thomas Chen for sending me his insightful and thorough dissertation on Chinatown. Thanks to Adam Gaffin for all his work on Universal Hub and the staff of The History Project and the Northeastern University Archives, and to Aaron Schmidt of the Boston Public Library. Thanks to Frank Bellotti, Mike Ingeme, Brother Ralph, John J. Spurr Jr., Doug Meyer, and Judy Farrar.

I don't know what I would have done without my first editor and toughest critic, Florence Schorow. I must also thank my Medford writer's group for enduring numerous drafts of this manuscript, Anne Stuart for reading a first draft, and the ROMEOs for sharing their memories. A huge thank you to Caitlin Dow for her editing and Shelby Larsson for her support. Words are inadequate to express my gratitude to Union Park Press Publisher Nicole Vecchiotti for suggesting this topic and supporting me through the book's long birth.

SOURCES

Publications:

Angier, Roswell, *"A Kind of Life:" Conversations in the Combat Zone*, Danbury, N.H.: Addison House, 1976.

Berson, Jessica, *The Naked Result: How Exotic Dance Became Big Business*, New York: Oxford University Press, 2015.

Chen, Thomas C. (2014). "Remaking Boston's Chinatown: Race, Space, and Urban Development, 1943-1994," (Doctoral dissertation, Brown University).

Carpenter, Teresa, *Missing Beauty: A True Story of Murder and Obsession*, New York: W.W. Norton, 1988.

Johnson, Eithne and Schaefer, Eric, "Quarantined! A Case Study of Boston's Combat Zone," from *Hop on Pop: The Politics and Pleasures of Popular Culture*," edited by Henry Jenkins III, Tara McPherson, Jane Shattuc, editors, Duke University Press, January, 23, 2003.

Finkelstein, M. Marvin, "The traffic in sex-oriented materials," United States Commission on Obscenity and Pornography. *Technical Report of the Commission On Obscenity And Pornography*, volume 5, (Washington: 1971).

Giorlandino, Salvatore M. (1986). "The Origin, Development, and Decline of Boston's Adult Entertainment District: The Combat Zone," (Master's thesis, Massachusetts Institute of Technology).

Kennedy, Lawrence W., *Planning the City Upon a Hill: Boston Since 1630*, Amherst, M.A.: The University of Massachusetts Press, 1992.

Lewin, Lauri, *Naked is the Best Disguise: My Life as a Stripper*, London: Pandora, 1986.

Lynch, Kevin, *The Image of the City*, Cambridge, M.A.: MIT Press, 1960.

Preston, John, edited, *Flesh and the Word 2: An Anthology of Erotic Writing*, New York: Plume, 1993.

Tudan, Jonathan, *Lovers, Muggers & Thieves: A Boston Memoir*, Calabasis, C.A.: Hawk Nest Press, 2008.

Municipal documents:

"Boston's Adult Entertainment District," Boston Redevelopment Authority pamphlet, January 1976.

"Development Proposal for the Combat Zone: Police Analysis Exercise," Jean L. Cumming, John F. Kennedy School of Government, Harvard University, April 14, 1986.

"Gaiety Theater Study Report," Boston Landmarks Commission, undated.

Interim Report, Entertainment District Study, Boston Redevelopment Authority,

April 1974, Robert T. Kenney, director.

Lower Washington Street Area: A Program for Revitalization, City of Boston, June 1978.

"Midtown Cultural District Plan: A plan to manage growth," Boston Redevelopment Authority, 1988.

"Report of the Boston Landmarks Commission on the Potential Designation of the Boylston Building as a Landmark under Chapter 772 of the Acts of 1975," Boston Landmarks Commission, 1977.

"Report of the Boston Landmarks Commission on the Potential Designation of the Hayden Building as a Landmark under Chapter 772 of the Acts of 1975," Boston Landmarks Commission, 1977.

"Report of the Boston Landmarks Commission on the Potential Designation of the Liberty Tree Building as a Landmark under Chapter 772 of the Acts of 1975 as amended," Boston Landmarks Commission, 1985.

Theatre and Entertainment District report, Boston Redevelopment Authority, 1979.

Transcript of Zoning Commission hearing, September 11, 1974, prepared October 1, 1974.

· ·

Notes on Chapters

INTRODUCTION: The Liberty Tree

The quote from Billy Dwyer is from a January 21, 2016 interview; Liberty Tree history is from "Report of the Boston Landmarks Commission on the Potential Designation of the Liberty Tree Building under Chapter 772 of the Acts of 1975 as amended," 1985; and David Sears, "Liberty Tree Notes: From City Records, 1850," unpublished document, Bostonian Society. Development of Washington Street is from a Boston Landmarks Commission report on the Boylston Building. "It took balls" quote is from a February 24, 2016 interview with a former BRA official; the "vortex" quote is from a January 15, 2016 interview with Don Stradley. The acreage of the Combat Zone is variously described in newspaper accounts as five and a half, six, and seven acres. A BRA map indicates the area is closer to five and a half acres. Adult businesses in Park Square, while not in the AED, were considered part of the Combat Zone.

CHAPTER 1: It Really is a Combat Zone

Some attribute the name "Combat Zone" to the proliferation of military men who sought tailoring services from Chinese seamstresses. The first reference found is in the April 27, 1951 *Boston Traveler* newspaper article "Marine, sailor sentenced in Essex St. affray." Other details are from a series in the *Record American* from July to August 1964, which referenced "the so-called Combat Zone." Another early reference was in a September 20, 1964 *Boston Globe* article about the Rev. Billy Graham's visit to Izzy Ort's club. Description of 1950s downtown is based on a March 4, 2016 interview with former Boston Mayor Ray Flynn. Information on Boston's manufacturing, financial, and population decline is attributed to William Kennedy's *Planning the City Upon a Hill: Boston Since 1630*, chapter seven, "Collins, Logue, and the 'New Boston.'" Details on Boston's Chinese community are from Thomas Chen's authoritative dissertation, "Remaking Boston's Chinatown: Race, Space, and

Urban Development, 1943-1994." Background information also came from Jonathan Kaufman's "From Scollay Square tattoo parlors to Combat Zone porno films," *Boston Globe*, December 27, 1984. Details on Izzy Ort come from Richard Vacca, *The Boston Jazz Chronicles*, and Ort's obituary by William Buchanan in the *Globe*, published October 14, 1975. Information on Boston's theaters comes from a city report on "Lower Washington St. Area: A Program for Revitalization."

CHAPTER 2: **From Scollay Square to the Combat Zone**

I am indebted to David Kruh's book *Always Something Doing*, and to numerous conversations with Kruh for insight into Scollay Square. Background on Collins, Logue, and White is from Kennedy's *Planning the City Upon a Hill*. Other details on Logue are from the December 24, 1965 *Life* magazine article, "Boston Gladiator: Ed Logue." The "halving" of the Chinese Merchant Association building is described in Chen's dissertation; Ann Corio details come from Dick Sinnott, "These stripteasers strutted with style," *Boston Globe,* March 28, 1999. The Tony Pasquale information is based on interviews with his son Mark Pasquale that took place on June 7, 2016 and August 6, 2016. Angel Walker was interviewed August 23, 2016. The pornographic bookstore information comes from a remarkable study conducted by Boston University Law Professor Marvin M. Finkelstein, published in the 1971 report by the US Commission on Obscenity and Pornography. The early BRA history is based on a February 25, 2016 interview with Paul McCann and a February 24, 2016 interview with a former BRA official. Information on Mayor Kevin White is from White's January 28, 2012 obituary in the *Globe*. Sally the Shape story is from David O'Brian's article, "A Separate Peace, Sort Of," in the *Boston Phoenix*, July 11, 1978. Details of the Combat Zone's early days are from "The Combat Zone: An In-depth Report," *Globe*, July 31, 1966.

CHAPTER 3: **Porno Chic**

Sources include "The Porno Plague," *Time*, April 5, 1976. "Obviously, few issues trigger" quote is from Robert Taylor's August 3, 1969 article, "The politics of pornography in Boston," in the *Boston Globe*. Details on Sinnott come from his May 2, 2003 *Globe* obituary by Tom Long; "Sinnott Censors Musical," *Globe*, May 5, 1960; and "Fewer Jobs for Sinnott," *Globe*, May 8, 1962. "This is the time of porno chic" quote is from an August 6, 2016 interview with George Mansour. "In one fell swoop" and "a mecca of pornography" quotes are from Al Larkin's April 28, 1974 *Globe* article, "Porno ruling loosens up Combat Zone." "Zoning can prohibit" quote is from a February 25, 2016 interview with Paul McCann.

CHAPTER 4: **Creating an Adult Playground**

For this chapter, I relied heavily on Salvatore M. Giorlandino's 1986 dissertation, "The Origin, Development, and Decline of Boston's Adult Entertainment District." Information on Debra Beckerman comes from Bill Fripp's November 3, 1973 *Globe* article, "Tone for the Zone"; Adrian Taylor's September 30, 1974 article, "The Eroge-nous Zone and Other Sorrows," in *The Heights;* Al Larkin's September 13, 1973 *Globe* article "Combat Zone gets a PR Woman," *Globe*; and Dave O'Brian's July 5, 1977 arti-cle, "Banned in Boston Again? Plans to upgrade the Combat Zone have been an utter failure and there's plenty of blame to go around," in the *Boston Phoenix*, July 5, 1977; Kenney's "We have picked Liberty Tree" quote is from the *Herald American*, June 7, 1974. The "Conventioneers with money" quote is from the BRA's April 1974 "Enter-tainment District Study." The Dave Waller information is from a February 16, 2016 interview. The bookstore quote is from the Finkelstein study. The diGrazia assess-ment is from a January 21, 2016 interview with Billy Dwyer, a January 14, 2016 inter-view with Barney Frank, and interviews with Edward McNelley on January 27, 2016 and August 4, 2016. William F. Buckley Jr.'s commentary is from "Boston's Newest Arrangement with Sin," *Globe,* June 21, 1974. Barney Frank's biography details are from Elliot Friedman's April 4, 1968 *Globe* article, "Shoeless Barney Frank; Mayor White's Dynamo," and the March 21, 1974 Associated Press article, "Prostitution Is-sue Sparks Angry Debate." Ahern's 1973 quote "we would be unwise" is cited in Joe Keohane's November 2008 *Boston Magazine* article, "No Sin-Zone." The "erogenous zone" quote is from Ed Zuckerman's September 1976 *Oui* magazine article, "Boston Gets an Erogenous Zone." Direct quotes from the September 11, 1974, Boston Zoning Board meeting are from the hearing transcript. Chan's quotes are from a March 5, 2016 interview, and from Chen's dissertation, *Remaking Boston's Chinatown*. The in-formation about the *Globe's* AED support comes from a September 20, 1974 editorial, "Containing the Combat Zone," and Ian Menzies' October 17, 1974 column, "BRA right to contain Combat Zone." Other sources: Robert Jordan, "Boston board ap-proves zone for adult shows," *Globe*, November 15, 1974; Sam Allis, "This was where hookers, johns, and trouble met," *Globe*, March 7, 2010.

INTERMISSION: **The Politician and the Foxe**

Details of the Mills-Foxe affair come from the December 16, 1974 *Time* article, "The Fall of Chairman Mills," Lloyd Shearer's October 5, 1975 *Globe* article, "The Story Behind Fanne Foxe and Wilbur Mills," Mills' May 3, 1992 *New York Times* obitu-ary, "Wilbur Mills, Long a Power In Congress, Is Dead at 82," and Don Stradley's online post, "A few tales from the Pilgrim." Details on Savino come from Stradley, Kruh, and Ernie Santosuosso's *Globe* stories "Pilgrim Makes the Switch," May 28, 1973 and "Live Shows for new Pilgrim," January 24, 1973. The "Brighter than most" quote is from Jeremiah Murphy's November 19, 1974 *Globe* article, "That 'Pop' was champagne and/or Argentine Firecracker."

CHAPTER 5: **Girls, Girls, Girls**

Much of this chapter is based on interviews with Julie Jordan, January 28, 2016; Elizabeth T. Brawner "Kendra Wilde," January 26, 2016; Lauri Umansky "Lauri Lewin," February 2, 2016; Heidi "the champagne girl," January 11, 2016; Joel Fein-gold, January 26, 2016; Jonathan Tudan, January 30, 2016; and Lisa Treat, March 11,

2016. I also relied on Jessica Berson's book and conversations with her on January 15, 2015, as well as Lewin's book, *Naked is the Best Disguise.* Roswell Angier's photo essay book, *"A Kind of Life,"* provided a look at the strippers of the 1970s. Tudan's book *Lovers, Muggers & Thieves* gave insight into the hierarchy of women in the Zone. Information on Princess Cheyenne, who declined to be interviewed, came from Berson's book, *The Naked Result,* and several articles: "What's a nice girl like you doing in a place like this?" by Lucy Johnson (Cheyenne), *Boston Magazine,* April 1984; "Lucy was the Cat's Meow," *People,* August 20, 1979; "She saw light in the dark underbelly of Boston," by Lucy Wightman, *Patriot Ledger,* February 23, 2010; and "Exposed: Lucy Wightman," by Keith O'Brien, *Boston Globe Magazine,* January 22, 2006. "Reptile" quote is from John Kifner's December 4, 1976 *New York Times* article, "Boston 'Combat Zone' becomes target of police."

CHAPTER 6: **Dealing with the Devil**

The description of the pizza sign incident is based on a May 14, 2016 interview with John Sloan and O'Brian's, "Banned in Boston." Other background on Sloan is from Lee Grove's "Pornucopia: Essaying the way of all flesh," *Boston Magazine,* May 1976. Detroit's dispersal porn solution is cited by David Gumpert in the June 30, 1977 *Wall Street Journal* article "Problems in the Combat Zone"; the information about inquiries from other cities comes from Gumpert's January 6, 1976 *Wall Street Journal* article, "X-Rated Businesses in Boston are given home on the raunch." Robert T. Kenney material comes from his March 18, 2016 obituary in the *Globe.* Information about the Liberty Tree park dedication comes from George McKinnon's June 11, 1975 *Globe* article, "City will snub park dedication." The "took down sign" quote is from McKinnon's June 13, 1975 *Globe* article, "Combat Zone dedicates park." Other sources: "Boston's Adult Entertainment District," Boston Redevelopment Authority pamphlet, January 1976; Fripp, "One 15,000 gallon milk bottle, please," *Globe,* April 21, 1977; Robert Campbell, "The Chinese Gate Caper," *Globe,* October 30, 1977 and Campbell, "They're out to get the Combat Zone," *Globe,* April 16, 1978; David Farrell, "Combat Zone headed for trouble," *Globe,* March 2, 1975; and Richard Hudson, "Combat Zone plan: shrink it," *Globe,* August 22, 1977.

INTERMISSION: **The Patriot Stripper**

The Hedy Jo Star information is from Berson's book, *The Naked Result.* Other information is from interviews with Julie Jordan and Peter Bates, February 20, 2016.

CHAPTER 7: **The Seduction of Mayor White**

The description of White's Zone visit is based on John B. Wood's hilarious February 9, 1975 *Globe* story: "Incognito Mayor finds Boston nightlife lively." The description of the prostitute roundup is based on interviews with Billy Dwyer and McNelley and Bob Sales' November 27, 1974 *Globe* article "X-Rated Night on the Town was just Part of His Job."

CHAPTER 8: **Not Supposed to Happen**

Details on the Puopolo case are based on interviews with Danny Puopolo, Francesca Sciaba, and Jan Brogan on March 21, 2016, and subsequent interviews with Brogan. O'Neil's quote about "The creation of the Zone" is from David O'Brian's December 19, 1976 *Herald American* article, "Smut's a gray area." The "Adam 12" information is from Richard J. Connolly's October 5, 1976 *Globe* article, "His unfinished task of reform." Information about diGrazia's corruption report is from Connolly's November 9, 1976 *Globe* article, "Downtown police corruption alleged." "The nightmare was Harvard's" article by Joe Concannon appeared in the *Globe* on November 14, 1976. The information about Harvard's "drubbing" is from Robin M. Peguero's June 8, 2005 *Harvard Crimson* article, "Stabbing Shocks Campus." Arrest records from Allen, Easterling, and Soares are from Boston Police Department documents. The sequence of events of early November 16, 1976, is drawn from newspaper accounts, Boston Police Department records and witness statements, and, in particular, *Commonwealth v. Soares*, 377 Mass. 461, Mass. Supreme Court (1979). The "Make me a miracle," quote is from Eleanor Roberts' December 12, 1976 *Herald American* article, "The Puopolo family still hopes for Andy." The Flynn quote about "Whose rights are we protecting" is from Earl Marchand's November 20, 1976 *Herald American* article, "Civic drive swells to scour Zone." Beckerman's "whipping boy," quote is from Jeremiah Murphy's December 15, 1976 *Globe* article, "… But things are the same." The quote about a flower being cut down is from the December 18, 1976 Associated Press article "Our prayers are just beginning." The joint enterprise is described by Alan H, Sheehan in "Lawyers dispute reason for attack on Puopolo," *Globe*, March 23, 1977. Trial descriptions are from the following articles: Sheehan, "Puopolo witness describes chase, fights," *Globe*, March 17, 1977; Alex MacPhail, "Puopolo slay witness feared for his own life," *Herald American*, March 19, 1977; Sheehan, "Defendant admits he stabbed Puopolo," *Globe*, March 22, 1977. The "I burn up" quote is from Roberts' March 20, 1977 *Herald American* article, "Slain Harvard athlete family," The "If it had been" quote is from Owens' artile, "3 guilty in Puopolo case get life terms, no parole," *Globe*, March 25, 1977. More information comes from Joseph Harvey's March 8, 1979 *Globe* article, "Convictions overturned in Puopolo murder case."

CHAPTER 9: **Danger Zone**

Details on the Robin Benedict murder come from Teresa Carpenter's book, *Missing Beauty*, and Michael K. Frisby's November 1, 1983 *Globe* article, "A murder trial—with no body found." Other sources: Stradley's blog post, "Was There A Combat Zone Strangler?", and "Police have few clues in girl's murder," *Globe*, June 12, 1977. The details about the "Rita Owen" case come from a Billy Dwyer interview, Paul Langner's March 14, 1982 *Globe* article, "Zone prostitute gets life term," and Joseph Harvey's July 10, 1984 *Globe* artivle, "Mass. high court sets aside woman's murder conviction." *Globe*, July 10, 1984. "Money itself was an addiction" information is based on Jeremiah Murphy's June 16, 1977 *Globe* article "I hate the life but love the money."

CHAPTER 10: **The Constitution and the Combat Zone**

Based largely on interviews with Regina Quinlan on January 13, 2016, and subsequent conversations. Other sources include Teresa Hanafin's May 3, 1992 *Globe* article, "Convent to court in between, new judge defended adult-book sellers," and William Doherty's June 17, 1981 *Globe* article "City wrong on peep shows." The Goldings background is from John Yang's February 8, 1981 *Globe* article, "Whither Boston's Combat Zone," Richard H. Stewart's February 11, 1988 *Globe* article, "Lawyer Champions Rights," Thanassis Cambanis' July 18, 2002 *Globe* article, "Goldings sentenced to three years in prison," and Steven Marantz's May 10, 1989 *Globe* article, "Bumped by videos, Combat Zone business is grinding to a halt."

CHAPTER 11: **Unrepentant**

The "I knew it was all over," quote is from the Sloan interview. The "We were always opposed" quote by O'Neil is from O'Brian's "Banned in Boston." The information about the legality of nude dancing is from from O'Brian's December 19, 1976 *Herald American* article, "Smut's a gray area." The "assorted donuts" information is from an October 5, 1977 *Globe* article. Details on the licensing crackdown are from a March 4, 2016 interview with Diane Modica. Information on Beckerman's disappearance is from the August 31, 1977 *Globe* article, "Dancer-Publicist for Combat Zone Reported Missing," and O'Brian's September 6, 1977 *Phoenix* article, "Missing Person." The number of adult businesses in the Zone two years after the Puopolo murder is from Schaefer and Johnson's "Quarantined! A Case Study of Boston's Combat Zone." Combat Zone storefronts descriptions are based on archival footage posted in the Boston TV News Digital Library, http://bostonlocaltv.org, including December 6, 1976, December 15, 1976, February 15, 1977, May 31, 1978, June 1, 1978, and February 7, 1979. Juice bar information is from *Globe* articles published March 5, 1978 and February 8, 1979. Descriptions of gay experiences in the Zone are from Michael Bronski's "How Sweet (And Sticky) It Was," and Christopher Wittke's "Just Do It," chapters in *Flesh and the Word*. The quote about law enforcement's legal tango with pornographic films is from an interview with McNelley. A great source for club descriptions was Alan Richman's February 12, 1979 *Globe* article, "Combat Zone's expensive thrills." Details on Chinatown are from March 5, 2016 interviews with Frank Chin and Peter Chan. Other sources include Ray Richard's February 13, 1977 *Globe* article, "Pressure of the law closing Combat Zone clubs," and the BRA's 1979 "Theatre and Entertainment District" report.

CHAPTER 12: **Mobsters in the Zone**

Information on mob connections is based on a January 30, 2016 interview with Steven Nichols, a March 1, 2016 interview with Thomas Dwyer, and interviews with; McNelley and Billy Dwyer. Other details are from the *Globe* Spotlight series on organized crime and pornography, which ran from February 13 to February 18, 1983, written by Stephen Kurkjian, Thomas Palmer, Peter Mancusi, and researcher M.E. Malone. Palmer and Kurkjian were also interviewed by the author in January

2016. The quote about Teddy Venus making decisions for the Two O'Clock Lounge comes from O'Brian's "Banned in Boston." Other sources: Alan H. Sheehan's March 9, 1975 *Globe* article, "License board preparing charges against 3 downtown bars"; Ed Corsetti and Earl Marchand's December 17, 1976 *Herald American* article, "Organized crime big Zone investor"; Corsetti and Marchand's Decemeber, 19, 1976 *Herald American* article, "Killer reported meeting with Zone area bar owner"; Richard Connolly's January 11, 1976 *Globe* article, "Who runs the Mob in New England?"; Ed Quill's April 9, 1988 *Globe* article, "Woburn's Venios family reputed to have business ties to Angiulos." Details on Angiulo and Palladino are from the April 7, 1987 article "FBI foiled plan to kill witness," part of a *Globe* Spotlight series on organized crime. Details on the Venios brothers are from United States of America, Appellee, v. George M. Bucuvalas... v. Bel-art Realty, Inc., Defendant, Appellant, 970 F.2d 937 (1st Cir. 1992).

CHAPTER 13: With a Bang and a Whimper

Information on the VCR's impact comes from Marantz's May 10, 1989 *Globe* article, "Bumped by videos, Combat Zone business is grinding to a halt." Real estate prices are from Jonathan Kaufman's December 27, 1984 *Globe* article, "Real Estate Development Boom Threatens Adult Entertainment." Flynn's "You would have thought," quote is from an interview. The information about the Pussy Cat Lounge's auction is from Jane Meredith Adams' July 4, 1987 *Globe* article, "End of runway for Pussy Cat Lounge." Information on Chinatown's expansion comes from several articles: Steve Bailey's January 22, 2003 *Globe* article, "Which Way Chinatown," Peter S. Canellos' January 10, 1993 Associated Press article, "Chinatown clout vs. The Zone," and John King's August 16, 1987 Associated Press article, "Influx of Asians: Lucrative land changing in face of Boston's Combat Zone." The "Even organized crime" quote is from Geoffrey Rowan's April 20, 1986 *Boston Herald* article, "Five years after the sale" and the February 14, 1983 *Globe* article "Spotlight: The Pornography Industry." *Globe,* Feb. 14, 1983. Arrest numbers for prostitutes are from McNelley, cited in the July 20, 1989 *New York Times* article, "Boston Journal: Cleanup comes to the Combat Zone." Other development details are from a March 15, 2016 interview with Kevin Fitzgerald interview and several newspaper articles: Arlene Levinson's January 11, 1988 Associated Press article, "Red lights fade as Combat Zone loses battle against developers," Joe Sciacca and Jack Meyers' November 5, 1989 *Boston Herald* article, "Twilight of the Zone," Joan Vennochi's December 29, 1984 *Globe* article, "Cleanup poses its own problems," and the July 26, 1987 *New York Times* article, "Bostonians Hail Ebb of a Sex District." The Glass Slipper information is from the McCann interview and Camille Dodero's September 30, 2005 *Boston Phoenix* article, "Cinderella Story." For criticism of downtown development, see Adrian Walker's February 4, 1996 *Globe* article, "Two landmark buildings in the Combat Zone are soon to be demolished." Gaiety Theater information is from the Landmarks Commission report and Mark Leccese's October 27, 2002 *Globe* article, "The end of Gaiety?" The Hayden building information is from the Landmarks Commission

Report, Eric Moskowitz's June 2, 2012 *Globe* article, "Hayden Building, historic gem of the Combat Zone, to be restored," and a January 21, 2016 interview and site visit with Kathy Kottaridis, executive director, Historic Boston.

CHAPTER 14: Saying Goodbye to the Zone

Mark Pasquale, interview on site, August 6, 2016. A treasure trove of memories about the Combat Zone can be found on: www.universalhub.com, search: Combat Zone. For AED zoning, see: www.bostonplans.org,

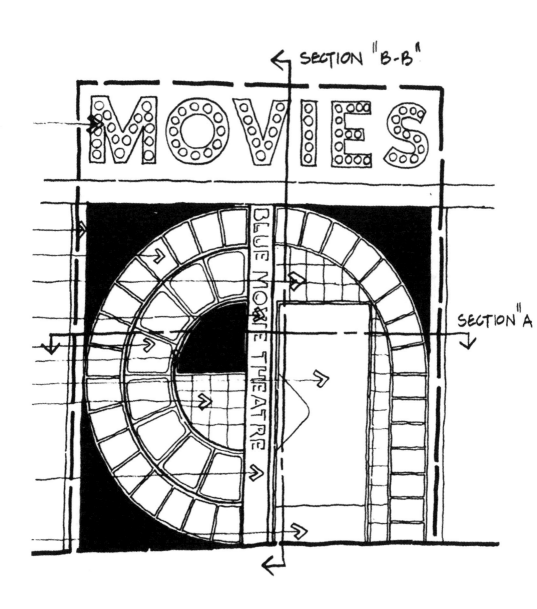

SECTION "B-B"

SECTION "A"

FACADE ELEVATION

INDEX

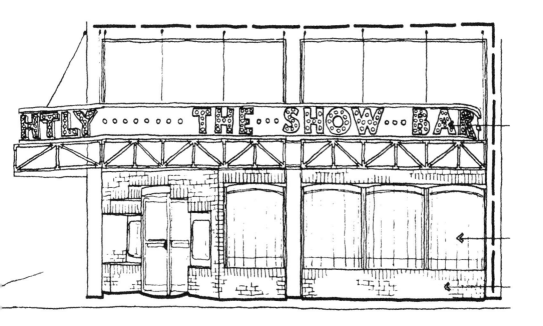

WASHINGTON ST. ELEVATION

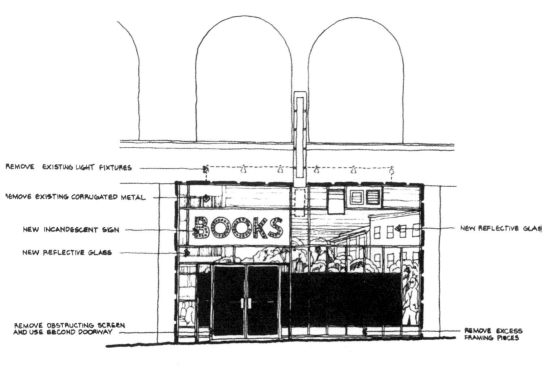

REMOVE EXISTING LIGHT FIXTURES

REMOVE EXISTING CORRUGATED METAL

NEW INCANDESCENT SIGN

NEW REFLECTIVE GLASS

NEW REFLECTIVE GLASS

BOOKS

REMOVE OBSTRUCTING SCREEN AND USE SECOND DOORWAY

REMOVE EXCESS FRAMING PIECES

FACADE ELEVATION
SCALE: 1/4" = 1'-0"

W – X – Y – Z

All images in the index are from *Boston's Adult Entertainment District*, a pamphlet produced by the Boston Redevelopment Authority in January 1976. Upon seeing the printed pamphlet, BRA director Kenney demanded a certain drawing be removed and the pamphlet reprinted. Courtesy City of Boston.

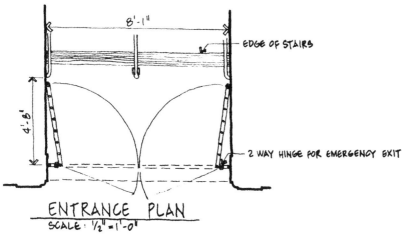

8'-1"

EDGE OF STAIRS

4'-8'

2 WAY HINGE FOR EMERGENCY EXIT

ENTRANCE PLAN
SCALE: ½" = 1'-0"

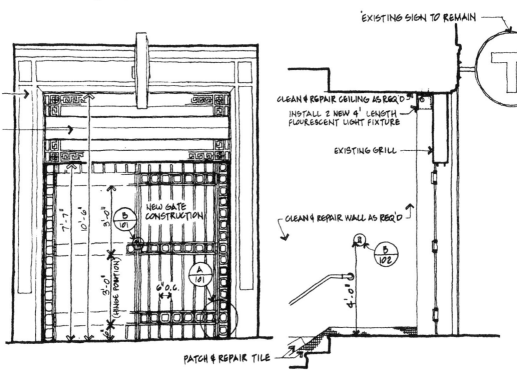

EXISTING SIGN TO REMAIN

CLEAN & REPAIR CEILING AS REQ'D

INSTALL 2 NEW 4' LENGTH
FLOURESCENT LIGHT FIXTURE

EXISTING GRILL

CLEAN & REPAIR WALL AS REQ'D

NEW GATE
CONSTRUCTION

7'-7"

10'-6"

3'-0"

3'-0"
(HINGE PORTION)

6" O.C.

B
101

A
101

B
B
102

4'-0"

PATCH & REPAIR TILE

ELEVATION
SCALE: ½" = 1'-0"

SECTION
SCALE: ½" = 1'-0"

ABOUT THE AUTHOR

STEPHANIE SCHOROW is the author of seven books on Boston history, including *Drinking Boston: A History of the City and Its Spirits*, *The Cocoanut Grove Fire*, *Boston on Fire*, *East of Boston: Notes from the Harbor Islands*, and *The Crime of the Century: How the Brink's Robbers Stole Millions and the Hearts of Boston*. She co-wrote *The Boston Mob Guide: Hit Men, Hoodlums & Hideouts* with Beverly Ford. She has worked as an editor and reporter for the *Boston Herald*, the Associated Press, and numerous other publications.